OUTLAW TRAILS
of Texas

OUTLAW TALES
of Texas

True Stories of the Lone Star State's
Most Infamous Crooks, Culprits, and Cutthroats

Second Edition

Charles L. Convis

TWODOT®

GUILFORD, CONNECTICUT
HELENA, MONTANA
AN IMPRINT OF GLOBE PEQUOT PRESS

To buy books in quantity for corporate use
or incentives, call **(800) 962–0973**
or e-mail **premiums@GlobePequot.com.**

Map by Daniel Lloyd © Morris Book Publishing, LLC
Project editor: Meredith Dias
Layout: Lisa Reneson

Library of Congress Cataloging-in-Publication Data is available on file.

ISBN 978-0-7627-7217-9

Printed in the United States of America

10 9 8 7 6 5 4 3 2 1

To the memory of Gray Golden

Her contributions to the Texas State Historical Society and to the Texas Genealogical Society, of which she was president in 1982–1983, have provided a lasting legacy to Texas and those who appreciate its history.

Contents

Acknowledgments

Many people deserve my gratitude for the help they provided, and I am pleased to acknowledge them here.

Mike Pacino at Cal Farley's Boys Ranch, Texas, provided much information about little-known events at Old Tascosa, where the ranch is located. Long known as the "Cowboy Capital of the Plains," the history of Tascosa's buffalo hunters and outlaws and lawmen such as Billy the Kid and Pat Garrett has almost obscured its history of sheepmen and one fascinating story about them.

Mary Ann Ruelas on the staff of the Panhandle-Plains Historical Museum in Canyon, Texas, welcomed me to do research and copy documents on a day the museum was closed to the general public.

Julia Putnam spent a half day driving me around old Fort Griffin in Shackelford County, Texas, and the land her grandfather, J. B. Putnam, bought in 1906 from J. A. Mathews, Mary Larn's brother. I enjoyed hearing Julia talk about the Old West's interesting characters who made Fort Griffin as fascinating a place as Dodge City, Virginia City, Tombstone, and Deadwood. Hopefully it will be restored; a start has been made. Julia's family property includes the three-room cabin at Camp Cooper that John Larn built for his new wife, soon to be a young widow. Just across the Brazos River is Julia's family home, which Larn built as his outlaw fortune increased. Behind is his grave.

Lenora Shelton opened her museum in Jacksboro, Texas, just for me. I admired her collection on Jack County history and the artifacts from the Warren Wagon Train Massacre.

County Judge Mitchell G. Davenport of Jack County spent an hour talking about the massacre and the history-making, but still mysterious, trials that followed. I wish he would write the story of the trials, though it would be difficult because the missing court records have never been recovered.

Marge Mack and other friendly deputies in the District Clerk's Office in McKinney, Texas, helped me find the record of marriage of Myra Belle Shirley (later Belle Starr, the Bandit Queen) and her first love, Jim Reed. Most writers call this an "alleged marriage," saying the record cannot be found.

Shelia Kmoch and Pauline Wachsmann, deputy clerks of the District Court of Lee County, Texas, located the original court records of the William P. Longley murder trial and judgment.

Preservation Officer John Anderson and the courteous staff of the Texas State Library in Austin produced helpful images and information from their records.

Archivist Katherine Salzmann and Assistant Archivist Tina Ybarra in the Alkek Library of Texas State University in San Marcos helped me find needed information in their extensive John Wesley Hardin collection.

Stephanie Langenkamp, director of the San Marcos City Library, found material to convince me that Myra Shirley Reed hid out in San Marcos while her husband, Jim, and three of his gang held up the San Antonio–Austin stage just outside town at the crossing of the Blanco River.

Jane Hoerster, chair of the Mason County, Texas, Historical Commission, located a picture of Callie Lewis, John Wesley Hardin's second wife (for a few hours). Jane's mother knew Callie well, and Jane told me that her mother had often told her that Callie did not want to talk about her marriage to Hardin.

Sally Perry, librarian at the Reeves County Library in Pecos, Texas, helped me find important information about Jim Miller.

Virginia Davis, archivist of the El Progreso Library, Archives, and Museum in Uvalde, Texas, and Lydia Steele, District Clerk of the 38th Judicial District of Texas, also in Uvalde, were very kind. Ms. Steele helped me pore over pages and pages of court records, many of which were undated and some of those that were had not been bound in chronological order.

David Hamblin, reference librarian for the Longview, Texas, Public Library, capably filled in for their archivist who was on vacation. The staff at the Gregg County, Texas, Historical Museum graciously allowed my wife to photograph firearms in their display cases.

Peggy O'Neill, my editor and a native of Austin, helped much with her comments and suggestions. Working with her and with Kaleena Cote and Meredith Rufino, both editors at Globe Pequot, was a great pleasure. They helped move the original manuscript and the revisions forward to completion.

I also appreciate Bob Kadoyama's suggestions, which helped me write a part of the introduction that I found difficult.

Most will find few—or perhaps no—heroes in this book. Texas had many heroes. No pioneer woman anywhere showed more courage and determination than nineteen-year-old Mathilda Friend of Legion Valley who, grievously wounded and scalped, single-handedly fought off fifty raiding Comanches. Three weeks later her husband had to lift her slumping forehead from her eyes so she could see the healthy baby girl she had just birthed. No soldier anywhere showed more bravery, loyalty, and nobility than Albert Sidney Johnston, the only man to serve as a general in three different North American armies, including that of the Republic of Texas. Finally, it would be hard to find a government leader showing more love for family, nations, and state than Sam Houston.

But this book is about outlaws; there are few, if any, heroes here.

Introduction

Cannibals ate all but four of Texas's first visitors. This event started three and a half centuries of violence that we know about, culminating in the last half of the nineteenth century, the period in which these stories take place. It should not be surprising that some of them reek with hatred and drip with gore.

The word "outlaw" in Texas history is not set apart by a firm line between right and wrong. As with other pages of Old West history, whether a gunman is a lawman or an outlaw sometimes depends on the story being told, and the Texas picture is even murkier. Violence in Texas developed around conflicts between groups that often defied racial and ethnic definitions.

The first and longest conflict was between Native Americans and the first settler-invaders. The land that became Texas was peopled mostly by Comanches, Apaches, and Kiowas, as warlike and determined to resist occupation by foreigners as Indians anywhere. Most western states solved their Indian "problem" in ten to twenty years; Texas needed fifty. For a quick look at this period of Texas history consider that the Texas frontier, which had slowly moved west over the years, suddenly bounced back a hundred miles during the Civil War when soldiers went east to fight.

But Texas also had peaceful Indians, such as the Caddoes. When most whites in Texas wanted to kill all Indians, other whites led the Caddoes to safety across the Red River into Indian Territory. The killing of the rescue leader by other vengeful whites for allowing the Indians to "escape" illustrates the murky Texas picture about violence. The complication goes even deeper. Most of the first settlers were Anglo-Saxon, but they also included free blacks, French, Spanish, and Mexicans who, themselves, had Indian blood.

Sometime between the Texas War of Independence in 1835–36 and the United States War against Mexico in 1846–47, many Texans began to look at Mexican people as a separate ethnic group. One Texas Ranger said in 1856 that he had less difficulty killing a Mexican than he did crushing a louse picked off his own body. At the same time Mexican newspaper editors called Texas Rangers "monsters who have been vomited from hell, thirsting to rape our beautiful damsels."

The reputation of Texas Rangers as defenders of law and order became mythology in Texas. We don't know what the Indians thought—they had no newspapers or books—but Mexicans on both sides of the border thought Rangers had all the sensitivity of rattlesnakes. It would take some time to cool that conflict down.

One of the people mentioned here started his battle against society by killing blacks. When Texas won its independence from Mexico, it had less than a thousand slaves and also some free blacks. In fact several black slaves won their freedom as a reward for their bravery in the battle in which Texas won that independence. Texas soon forgot its black patriots, and east Texas became a strong slave-holding region. But the racial problem was still more complex: Two-thirds of the state had practically no black slaves, and Sam Houston, an ardent Unionist, resigned as governor in protest of the legislature's illegal adoption of the constitution that brought it into the Confederacy.

Young Bill Longley's decision to kill blacks willy-nilly seems to have had more to do with perceived power over people he considered contemptible than with racial division. These roots of violence were not pervasive enough in Texas and the oppression hadn't lasted long enough at that time to be attributed to racial conflict. Longley certainly hated white Yankee soldiers as much as he hated black Texans.

Here's a short summary of the chapters, in order, starting with John Wesley Hardin.

Family Man. After being shot by a lying sheriff and learning that his innocent brother had been hanged by a vigilante mob, Hardin, named by his Methodist preacher father for the founder of his denomination, fled the state. By his own count, Hardin had just killed his fortieth man, and a $4,000 reward led to his arrest in Florida where he was hiding with his wife and their two babies, the youngest only eight days old. His father-in-law's bitterness and his brother-in-law's treachery contributed to his conviction and twenty-five-year sentence.

Hardin won release after fourteen years, during which he attended Sunday school and studied law. He started law practice, but his faithful wife who had stuck with him all those years had died, and life went downhill. After a one-night marriage with a fifteen-year-old girl, Hardin moved to El Paso and took up the defense of Jim Miller, a cousin's close friend.

Complications with a client who hired Hardin to represent her husband, and with the policeman who arrested her, led to the policeman's father hunting Hardin down like a dog, and shooting him from behind. Hardin had not killed anyone since he had been out of prison. With the top of his head blown off in an El Paso bar, his adult (he started killing at age fifteen) record of homicide-free months would stand at seventeen.

Family Troubles. Mary Matthews, youngest of the nine Matthews girls, fell in love with John Larn at first sight. He had already driven a trail herd to Colorado when he appeared at the Matthews Ranch on the Clear Fork of the Brazos, near Fort Griffin. He didn't tell Mary Matthews about the rancher, the sheriff, or the Mexicans he had killed on the trail drive. Mary's father had heard, though, and he and his wife tried to stop the wedding, but Mary had a will to match her beauty and the wedding went ahead.

Neighbors wondered about the increase in Larn's cattle herd, but he had been a leader in the Fort Griffin vigilantes and community respect got him elected sheriff. He appointed as deputy John Selman, who one day would kill John Wesley Hardin. But Larn resigned after one of his ranch hands was killed in a shoot-out by another of his deputies.

Rumors about Larn's rustling continued, and further shootings led to Larn's arrest and incarceration in the Albany jail. Some said he was ready to identify vigilantes.

On Sunday night, June 23, 1878, Larn lay down to get some sleep. He knew Mary was trying to get a lawyer and was sleeping, just across the village square, with their four-year-old son Will at her side. Then he heard the tramp of the vigilantes, and the guards agreeing to go outside and study the stars. In spite of their masks, Larn recognized his two brothers-in-law, married to Mary's sisters. The fusillade woke Mary, and she screamed into the night.

Death Dances on the Border. John Selman fled Shackelford County the night John Larn was killed, leaving his pregnant wife and their four children. She died birthing the next child. After fighting in the Lincoln County War in New Mexico, Selman showed up in Chihuahua with Nicanora, a woman who had found him in Mexico near death from smallpox with a line of buzzards waiting nearby.

After learning in 1888 that the Shackelford County rustling charges had been dismissed, Selman returned to El Paso and, four years later, joined the police force. He had a shoot-out with a former Texas Ranger named Bass Outlaw in which Outlaw was killed. By this time John Wesley Hardin was in El Paso, and the stage was set for a bewildering series of events.

Selman's close friend, Deputy United States Marshal George Scarborough, killed fugitive Martin Morose, certainly the West's strangest cowboy. Morose's wife had retained Hardin to represent her in getting her husband back from Mexico. Selman killed Hardin, Scarborough killed Selman, and Scarborough was killed by someone in Butch Cassidy's Wild Bunch four years to the day after he killed Selman. None of it made sense, but it eliminated some violent men from Texas.

Born to Hang. Jim Miller, John Wesley Hardin's cousin by marriage, never smoked, drank, or swore. He attended church so often he was called "Deacon Jim," but he had killed his grandparents when he was eight. Nine years later he left a church service, galloped three miles to his brother-in-law's house, shot him in the head as he slept, and got back before the service ended. Too young to be prosecuted for his first killing, he got an acquittal for his second.

After three more killings, all resulting in acquittals, Miller began charging for his work. His standard fee was $150 each, but when he killed Pat Garrett, the legendary lawman who had himself killed Billy the Kid twenty-five years before, he charged $1,500. Again he got an acquittal.

In 1908 Miller went to Ada, Oklahoma, to earn his highest fee, $2,000. This time a nephew gave him away, but the citizens of Ada didn't wait for a trial. They hanged him in a stable with three others, all at the same time.

A Foolish Boast. Kiowa chief Satanta's inclusion here might seem surprising, as Indians were considered to be at war with the United States, not lawbreakers subject to court prosecution. Apparently the only Indian chief ever prosecuted in a criminal court, Satanta was found guilty of murder—wrongfully, as it turned out—and the court records disappeared and have never been found.

The Texas governor reduced Satanta's death sentence to life at hard labor. Eventually released on parole, Satanta was returned to court for a parole violation—this time rightfully—and sent back to prison. Despondent, the fifty-five-year-old former chief, called the "Patrick Henry of the Indians," killed himself inside the prison.

Misdirected Vengeance from "Those Californians." Sostenes L'Archévèque vowed to kill every white man he could when he grew up. When the Casner brothers found California gold and invested it in sheep, they trailed them back to the Texas Panhandle, where L'Archévèque killed them and their herder for sheer pleasure. Charles Goodnight, just getting started in cattle ranching nearby, found the other brother and their father and told them what happened. By the time the relatives arrived, Colás Martínez, friend of Goodnight and brother-in-law of L'Archévèque, had killed his sister's husband to stop the spread of evil.

The father and brother swore vengeance on everyone involved in the murders of the brothers. But they did not understand what had happened since, and who had killed the killer. So they killed Colás, who had killed L'Archévèque, and hanged two others who had been present and supported the killing of their brothers' killer. Mexican sheepmen moved back to New Mexico and left Texas alone.

He Was a Man before He Was Done Being a Boy. Bill Longley, whom Believe-It-or-Not Robert Ripley claimed had been hanged three times, may have been Texas's most interesting outlaw. Not a robber or cattle rustler and never part of a gang, he got pure enjoyment out of the act of killing. When he was barely fifteen in 1866, a black policeman drew his gun and insulted Longley's father.

"You put that gun down," Longley demanded, drawing his own gun.

The policeman pointed his gun at Longley, and Longley shot him dead. Within a year Longley had killed at least three and probably five more black men. Longley continued to kill blacks, both former slaves and Yankee soldiers.

Once, vigilantes captured Longley and a horse thief as they sat by their fire and hanged them. But the celebration gunfire as the vigilantes rode away cut Longley's rope in two, and he survived.

Longley was thinking about settling down in Bandera County when he learned that a friend, Lon Sawyer, was scheming with the sheriff to turn him in for a reward. Longley got himself deputized by another sheriff and set out to capture Sawyer. After one of the West's wildest gun battles, involving carbines, pistols, and shotguns, plus horses and a pack of dogs, Sawyer lay dead, along with his horse and five of his dogs.

Longley had scored thirteen hits with eighteen shots. Sawyer fired fourteen times and only killed Longley's horse.

Longley was sentenced to hang in September 1878. He protested that it was unfair as he had only killed thirty-two men, and John Wesley Hardin killed more and only got a life sentence.

The noose slipped, and Longley dropped to his knees. But the sheriff boosted him up for his third hanging, and this one worked.

A Woman Who Saw Much of Life. Myra Belle Shirley grew up pretty, with a fiery temper and a hatred for Yankee soldiers. She became one of the West's leading women outlaws, known as Belle Starr in Indian Territory, but her earlier exploits in Texas are more interesting.

When Myra was fourteen, she fell in love with Jim Reed, two years older and one of Quantrill's Raiders. After the Civil War, the Shirley family moved to Texas to farm near Dallas, and Myra married Jim in 1866 after the Reeds moved to adjoining Collin County.

In 1874 Myra helped her husband lead one of Texas's most notorious stage robberies. Later that year Reed was killed by an acquaintance, and Myra eventually moved to Indian Territory for a more well-known, but not more interesting, career in crime.

Two Cities Give Up the Wild West. A wild shootout involving two famous gunmen in San Antonio's Harris Variety Theatre in March 1884 turned both Austin and San Antonio away from their Old West behavior. Ben Thompson, ex-Ranger, ex-prison inmate, soldier of fortune, and gambler, had been a popular city marshal (police chief) of Austin. The other gunman, John King Fisher, had also served time in prison and then organized a six-county gang operating along the Rio Grande in south Texas. At the time of the shoot-out he was sheriff of Uvalde County.

Just two years earlier, Thompson had killed Jack Harris, himself a soldier of fortune and policeman, and also part owner of the Harris Variety Theatre. Thompson, Austin city marshal at the time, tendered his resignation since no part of his duties included shooting policemen in another county. The Austin city council gave him a leave of absence instead and celebrated his acquittal at the trial. San Antonio citizens felt differently; so did Fisher, as he was Harris's friend.

On March 11 Sheriff Fisher and Thompson, for some unknown reason, went to the Harris Variety Theatre to see a vaudeville show. Probably no gun battle in Texas had so many witnesses or so many conflicting accounts of what happened. When it ended, one of the theater's owners lay dying, and Thompson and Fisher were both dead.

Austin newspapers raged, claiming an ambush. The San Antonio coroner's jury said three shots had hit Thompson. An Austin autopsy found eight shots in him. But citizens in both cities realized that it was best to say goodbye to the ways of the Old West, and both cities did.

Two Friends in the Hoo Doo War. The rugged Hill Country west of Austin was the battleground in the 1870s of the Hoo Doo War between German farmers and stockmen who adopted vigilante methods to fight what they called "American outlaws." The "American outlaws" saw themselves as cattlemen trying to make a living in a harsh land and relying in vain on officials to enforce the law.

Into this turmoil and madness rode Scott Cooley and his friend John Ringo. Cooley, an Indian fighter and ex-Ranger by the time he was nineteen, had once skinned an Indian, saying he would make a quirt from the hide. Ringo, related by marriage to Jesse and Frank James and the Younger brothers, was an avid reader of good books and a crack shot by the time he was twelve.

Early in the war, Cooley killed Johann Wohrle, Mason County deputy sheriff, who had, himself, once set up a cattleman prisoner by shooting his horse and leaving him to be killed by a vigilante mob. Cooley carried Wohrle's scalp in his pocket until he died, probably from poison.

Cooley and Ringo were once arrested and lodged in the Travis County jail in Austin at the same time that John Wesley Hardin was there. Hardin complained about being in the same jail with such a vicious prisoner as Ringo.

In January 1877, the Mason County courthouse burned and, with it, all records of the Hoo Doo War. Ringo went to Arizona and became a leader of the anti-Earp faction. His death from having the top of his head shot off was a final mystery in a mysterious life. It appeared that part of his scalp had been removed with a knife.

Border Bandits. Almost a million Texas cattle disappeared into Mexico from 1850 to 1875. Juan Nepomuceno Cortina, whose mother came from a distinguished family in Spain, was the main cause. He couldn't read and never signed his name until he became governor of Tamaulipas. In 1875, the year Cortina left Texas for good, Gregorio Cortez Lira was born. Cortez's courage, humility, and endurance made him even more of an icon to Mexicans in Texas than Cortina had been.

An unnecessary shooting on June 12, 1901, resulting from a sheriff's interpreter not knowing the difference in Spanish between "stallion" and "mare," led to Cortez's escape attempt that was almost Homeric in scope and detail. He was finally captured after he had traveled ten days on foot and on the backs of three small mares for hundreds of miles in south Texas with hundreds of peace officers trailing.

After eight trials, mostly with an Anglo lawyer from Gonzales and with help from sheriffs keeping mobs at bay, Cortez began serving a life sentence. But the lawyer refused to give up and twelve years later got his client a pardon.

Rest and Recuperation in Texas. The Wild Bunch, the Old West's largest gang, committed no crimes in Texas as far as we know, but they used Fannie Porter's brothel in San Antonio for rest and relaxation after their many holdups and robberies elsewhere. No detective thought of looking for them in San Antonio's most famous brothel. After they held up a bank in Winnemucca, Nevada, in 1900, they met in Fort Worth on their way to Porter's and had a photograph made showing all of them in derby hats. A Pinkerton detective recognized some of the men, and the search for them started in Texas.

At their last rendezvous at Porter's, the men all cheered while Butch Cassidy rode a bicycle up and down the street, a scene repeated in a movie about the gang.

Some of Porter's girls formed relationships with members of the gang. The longest was that between Etta Place and Harry Longabaugh (the Sundance Kid). Place went with the Sundance Kid and Butch Cassidy to South America. The three ranched for a time, and then the men returned to crime. We don't know what happened to Place.

Street Shoot-Out in Uvalde. John Daugherty only served as Uvalde County's sheriff for five months before he was killed. If you ask someone in Uvalde County, "Who was that famous sheriff from here?" you will always hear, "John King Fisher." Fisher deserved that notoriety, and his story is also to be found in these pages. But Daugherty's tale recounts an earlier, perhaps more interesting, time when the lives of settlers facing Indian "depredations" (the Natives probably had their own term) were complicated by their being thrust into an unpopular and—for Texas, at least—illegal Civil War.

Texas "joined" the Confederacy by adopting a new constitution, but the only way it could change the old constitution was by a popular vote of the people. When it became obvious that the people would not approve such a change, the legislature adopted the new constitution on their own, and the governor resigned in protest of the unlawful action.

Daugherty served as an officer in the Confederate cavalry but soon decided that he didn't think much of the war. Back home, the few Federal troops could not protect the settlers as the local men marched off to war. Daugherty's wife and children did the best they could. He returned from the war as a newly elected sheriff. In fact, he was elected while he was miles away, still serving in the cavalry. He brought with him his wife's two younger, newly orphaned sisters.

Five months later Daugherty was shot dead in a Uvalde street. How his pregnant wife, with four of her own children and two younger sisters to care for, got through the next seven months is a story to remember.

A Good Man Gone Bad. The eight Dalton brothers, cousins of the Youngers, can be divided into two groups. Three soon became outlaws and terrorized Indian Territory and the adjacent areas until two of them were killed in a failed attempt to rob two banks in Coffeyville, Kansas, where the robbers were well known.

Four brothers were law-abiding and lived out most of their adult lives in California.

Bill Dalton started out with the latter group, and with the help of two of them, tried to convince his outlaw brothers to change their ways. He failed, and the story of that failure tells how a man, prominent in California politics, died like some "pitiable chicken thief" after he held up a Longview, Texas, bank. His feelings about the injustice of the way he and his brothers had been treated by the law had turned him into an outlaw.

Family Man

On May 26, 1874, John Wesley Hardin joined his wife, Jane, and their fifteen-month-old daughter Mollie in Comanche, Texas, to celebrate his twenty-first birthday by watching the horse races. The Comanche County sheriff liked Hardin, a light-complected man with blue eyes who was five feet, ten inches tall. They enjoyed playing cards together in the local saloons. Deputy Sheriff Charles Webb of adjoining Brown County was also in Comanche that day, and friends warned Hardin that Webb wanted him dead or alive.

"Do you have papers for my arrest?" Hardin asked Webb.

"I don't know you," Webb lied. He had been studying Hardin's pictures for weeks.

"My name is John Wesley Hardin."

"So I know who you are, but I don't have arrest papers," Webb lied again.

"Then let's go in this saloon and take a drink."

When Hardin turned his back on Webb to enter the saloon, a friend shouted, "Look out, Wes!"

Later, Ranger N. A. Jennings would write that Hardin, with a six-shooter in each hand, could "with lightning rapidity put twelve bullets in a playing card at twenty yards." This time Hardin whirled, cross-drawing his revolvers from the holsters on his chest. Webb's bullet struck first, hitting Hardin in the side, but Hardin's killed Webb instantly with a head shot. Hardin, a careful counter, said Webb was the fortieth man he had killed.

Hardin fled, and irate citizens forgot that the deputy sheriff had tried to shoot Hardin in the back after denying that he had arrest papers. A vigilante mob then hanged Hardin's brother Joe, a completely innocent man.

Texas Rangers, Pinkerton detectives, and assorted gunmen seeking the $4,000 reward combed Texas for Hardin, but three years passed before the Rangers found him in Pensacola, Florida, and brought him back for trial. By that time he and Jane had a son, John Wesley Junior, and another daughter, Jennie, born eight days before the Rangers took her father away. The Comanche County jury found him guilty, and the judge gave him twenty-five years. Now Hardin sat in the Travis County jail in Austin, waiting for a decision from the Texas Court of Criminal Appeals.

Jane's brother, Brown Bowen, waited in the same jail for the appellate decision on his murder conviction in Gonzales County. Brown had killed Tom Halderman just before Christmas 1872 in a country store. Hardin was with him shortly before the killing, and he had helped his brother-in-law escape from the Gonzales County jail. The Rangers found Brown about the same time that they found Hardin, and his jury in Gonzales found him guilty at the same time that Hardin was found guilty in Comanche County.

The few meetings of the brothers-in-law, waiting in the Travis County jail, were not happy ones. First, Brown's carelessness had led to the Texas Rangers finding Hardin in Florida and Brown in Alabama. Jane's brother had betrayed Hardin's whereabouts in a letter to his (and Jane's) father, Neal Bowen, which the Rangers intercepted.

Second, Brown Bowen had the nerve to complain that Hardin only got twenty-five years for killing a sheriff while he got the death penalty for killing a no-account drunk. Halderman had just happened to be in the store that day, he had had too much to drink, and was passed out behind the stove when Bowen, out of pure spite, shot him in the back.

Third, it had been Hardin who smuggled the iron file into the jail shortly after Brown's arrest, who pried off his handcuffs after Brown cut through the bars, and who helped him escape to Florida and Alabama where the Bowens had kinfolks. In spite of that assistance, Brown's carelessness had led to Hardin's arrest and Brown's turning against his brother-in-law.

Fourth, and even more invidious, Brown Bowen and his father tried to cast doubt on Brown's conviction by laying the blame on Hardin.

"Why not tell the Rangers you killed Halderman?" Brown asked. "You already got a twenty-five-year sentence to serve. One more conviction won't mean much."

"Besides," Neal added, "you've got a lot of friends down in Gonzales. You might get off."

"They had the eyewitness," Hardin said, looking at Brown with contempt. "He saw you shoot the sleeping drunk in the back."

"But don't forget," Brown insisted, "you know how to get out of that poor excuse for a jail in Gonzales. You even escaped from it once yourself."

Hardin tried to conceal his contempt of his brother-in-law. He had never trusted him. But Jane's father had never treated him badly. He'd do his best to keep harmony in the family, but he wasn't going to admit to a killing he had nothing to do with. God knows, Texas and some of those other places had enough killings that he *did* do if they just wanted another one to charge. He looked directly at his father-in-law.

"You can't ask me to make a false statement, Neal. It wouldn't be honorable. They'd see through it. They had the eyewitness, you know."

In his pleas to the governor and to the public through the newspapers, Brown Bowen still claimed innocence and that John Wesley Hardin had shot Halderman.

Later, in answering a question by a newspaper reporter, Hardin was more blunt. "I've never killed a man the way Tom Halderman was killed. He was asleep. He had no chance to defend himself."

Neal, embittered that Hardin wouldn't take the blame for his son's crime, went before the grand jury at Cuero and told about Hardin's 1873 killing of J. B. Morgan. Hardin had never denied that killing, claiming self-defense. He had never been charged, but now, on the complaint of his father-in-law, he was indicted for another murder.

Hardin kept Jane informed of the family struggles, and Jane had always stood by him. He wrote, "You can rest assured that Brown and your father are not our friends but have done all they can against me. I am sorry for Brown's condition and yet it is only justice. . . . He has tried to lay his foul and disgraceful crimes on me."

Shortly before Brown's scheduled hanging, Neal and another daughter, Matt, visited Hardin in jail.

"Couldn't you make some statement, Wes," Neal pleaded, "something that would save Brown?"

"Not an honorable one. I don't think you'd want me to make a false one."

The day before the hanging, Matt came back to the jail, but Hardin refused to see her. She sent a note, pleading for some helpful statement. He replied: "For your sake, I would do anything honorable. I cannot be made a scapegoat. A true statement would do your brother no good and I won't make a false one."

On May 17, 1878, at the scheduled hour and before thousands of witnesses who packed the streets, Brown Bowen was hanged. Hardin wrote Jane that he had forgiven Brown for "his false and unfounded reports, and may God forgive him. Even after the cap (hood) was taken off, he said he was innocent, but that I had done it. Then he fell 7 feet and lived 7 seconds, witnessed by 4,500 people. May his poor soul be in peace and I hope that God forgives his sins. Kiss those darling babies for me once more and ever remember that I am ever your loving and true husband."

Old Neal Bowen took his son's body and buried it on the family farm in Coon Hollow. He didn't know that he dug the grave under the same oak tree where his daughter and Hardin had pledged their love five years before.

The appellate court affirmed Hardin's conviction, and he entered the Texas State Prison on October 5, 1878, to serve twenty-five years.

In spite of his pious statements about only telling the truth, even as a boy John Wesley Hardin had shown a callousness to some people, surprising in the light of his family and background. He was born in Bonham, Texas, on May 26, 1853, the second of eight children born to James and Elizabeth Hardin. His father, a circuit-riding Methodist preacher, named his son after the founder of his denomination. We know of nothing bad about his siblings, including the one killed by vigilantes.

When Hardin was eight, his father passed the bar examination and began teaching school and practicing law in Polk

County. John Wesley's cold-blooded heartlessness showed up early. In 1868, the fifteen-year-old boy killed his first victim, a former slave. At that time in east Texas, the community probably did not consider that the victim was a *former* slave, but Hardin fled, thinking he could not get a fair trial.

Later Hardin claimed that he had killed three soldiers who tried to arrest him and that neighbors and relatives helped him bury the evidence. Hardin always showed signs of intelligence, education, and fluency in language. His father sent him away in 1869 to teach school in Navarro County where other relatives lived. The sixteen-year-old soon left that for gambling and horse racing. By the end of that year he admitted that he had killed a freedman and four more soldiers.

In 1871, eighteen-year-old Hardin drove cattle to Abilene, Kansas. His cousin, Mannen Clements, was on the trail crew. On the drive up Hardin killed an Indian, who had shot an arrow toward him, and five Mexicans who were crowding the herd. When his cousin was jailed for killing two cowboys, Hardin arranged with Wild Bill Hickok for the cousin's escape. Later, after killing a man at his hotel, Hardin fled Abilene, fearing arrest by Hickok.

Eighteen-year-old Hardin married Jane Bowen on February 29, 1872, when he returned to Gonzales after the cattle drive. She would always be loyal to him, even though he was gone much of the time dodging arrest. Later in 1872, Hardin was arrested on a variety of indictments and lodged in the Gonzales County jail. This is when he broke out of jail with the help of Mannen Clements.

Hardin had killed Morgan in April 1873. That killing and the killing of Deputy Sheriff Webb were the only ones for which he was ever convicted.

After the Morgan killing, Hardin became embroiled in a famous Sutton-Taylor feud in south Texas as a leader of one faction, many of them his relatives. He helped kill the leader of the other side. Two months later came the shooting of Deputy Sheriff Webb in Comanche.

After Hardin's conviction for shooting Webb in October 1877, he was chained into a buggy with thirty pounds of iron around his neck, arms, and legs for transportation to Austin. A large crowd followed them out of town. Remembering what had happened to his brother Joe, Hardin was glad the Rangers had an armed escort for the first twenty miles. The crowd disappeared on the second day, and the prisoner breathed easier. When they Rangers reached Brushy Creek, fifty miles north of Austin, one of the Rangers rode down to the creek looking for a spring. He found one with a small, dark fortune-teller camped nearby. When the guard carried that news back to camp, Hardin told the Rangers that he believed somewhat in mystic powers and he would like to have his fortune told. They brought the gypsy up to their camp. He gazed into Hardin's eyes, turned Hardin's handcuffed hands up, and studied them carefully.

Finally the gypsy spoke in a low, quavering voice. "You've had a hard life, young man. You are going to the penitentiary for a long time. You will be a good man there and get out."

Then he paused as though finished.

"What then?" Hardin asked.

The dark little man closed his eyes as though not wanting to talk. Soon he continued, "I see grave trouble ahead for you. When you get out, you will kill two men. If you are not careful, you will be attacked from the back and killed."

A grim, gray look came to Hardin's eyes.

Callie Lewis Hardin at age fifteen.
Mason County, Texas, Historical Commission

The Rangers openly admired Hardin and treated him well. He had daring and skill with guns and horses. Many Rangers were not very tamed themselves. Soon after his return to Austin, Hardin wrote Jane, who was now back in Texas, "Dear, I had an ice cream treat today by the Rangers. I thought of our ice cream visits in New Orleans."

Jane hurried to Austin with the children, and for a short time while waiting for the mandatory appeal, the family had visits together in the Travis County jail. Jane's cheeks were pale and some sparkle had gone from her eyes, but both she and her husband remembered their pledges to stick together until death. That loyalty was severely tested by the conflict between Jane's husband and her father and brother. But Jane stayed true to her pledge and broke with her father.

Hardin tried several times to escape from prison. He never succeeded and drew severe punishment each time. Eventually he settled down, joined a debating society, began attending Sunday school, and studied law in prison. In 1888, ten years into his prison term, he wrote Jane, "I desire through you once more to make glad the hearts of our precious children by informing them that I, by the grace of God, still live. I still love them with that undying love that belongeth only to a true and devoted brave, but oppressed and exiled, father. I tell you that my deep, anxious solicitude for your welfare and their prosperity is unabating and that my love for you and them is so vast that it is boundless, so deep that it is unfathomable of that tenacious quality that neither time, vicissitudes, nor expatriation can impair, let alone sever. I but faintly outline the love that mellifluently flows from me to them to you that no vocabulary, no symbols, can describe, no sum of words define."

In January 1892, Hardin plea-bargained for a two-year con-current sentence for the Morgan killing. Jane Hardin died the next November. The children went to live with Fred Duder-stadt, a long-time friend of their father's who ranched nearby.

Hardin received a full pardon in February 1894. Although he had only served fourteen years and the early years had been marked with escape attempts and harsh punishments, his pardon recited that he had completed his sentence and was "behaving in an orderly manner." The gypsy on Brushy Creek had proved correct in one prediction: Hardin had been a good man in prison, at least after he gave up trying to escape.

Hardin joined his children in Gonzales, passed his bar examination, and began law practice there in October. He wished that Jane was with him to talk to Mollie when the twenty-one-year-old girl announced that she and Charley Bill-ings were getting married. Hardin tried in vain to get them to wait, thinking that Mollie was in too much haste. In the November 1894 election for sheriff, Hardin supported the man who lost by eight votes out of almost five thousand cast. The campaign had been bitter, and Hardin decided to leave before he got into trouble.

He moved west to Junction, where his brother Jeff lived. Hardin's son Johnny and daughter Jennie remained with Duderstadt. Hardin opened another law office, and in January 1895 he married fifteen-year-old Callie Lewis, daughter of a prominent rancher in Junction. Callie, just a few months older than Hardin's Jennie, left him on their wedding night.

In April 1895, after Hardin had given up any hope of recon-ciliation with Callie, he heard what amounted to a call of the clan from Pecos in West Texas. There, Jim Miller, a close friend and son-in-law of Mannen Clements, who was Hardin's cousin and close friend, had been shot in an unprovoked attack by George Frazer, the former sheriff. Hardin began preparing Miller's defense on rustling charges and was also hired to prosecute a criminal case against the former sheriff for shooting his client. The sheriff's case was moved to El Paso, and Hardin went there to handle it and finish the autobiography he was writing.

El Paso at that time was a safe harbor for evil. A hunted man could cross the river into Mexico or travel a few miles north to hide in the raw and lawless territory of New Mexico. El Paso was so overloaded with killers that the city hired Jeff Milton—perhaps Texas's greatest lawman—as its police chief.

Hardin had pleaded with his son Johnny to stay away from such places as El Paso, but Hardin opened a law office there. Milton warned his policemen that Hardin was the most dangerous man in America. As Hardin made the rounds of the saloons, men set up drinks, lost to him in poker, and tried desperately for friendship with such a famous gunman. They knew nothing about his self-education and reform in prison, and his later attempts to lead a law-abiding life.

One day, Mrs. Helen Morose called at Hardin's office. The husband of the over-painted woman—a prostitute in her younger days—had fled to Juarez, and Chief Milton sent word that he would be killed or jailed if he tried to return. Mrs. Morose wanted her husband back with protection from the law in El Paso. But she liked the looks of her new lawyer and soon forgot about Morose.

Jeff Milton didn't forget. When Morose tried to return, he was shot to death before reaching the Texas bank of the river. Mrs. Morose was soon known as "Wes Hardin's woman."

While Hardin was back in Pecos seeing about Miller's case there, Mrs. Morose went on a binge. Policeman John Selman Jr. arrested her, and she paid a $50 fine. Selman's father, an El Paso constable, had been a gunman in Fort Griffin thirty years before and a close associate of John Larn, another famous Texas outlaw.

When Hardin returned to El Paso and learned of the arrest of his new love, he became irate. "If I'd been here, you wouldn't have dared do that," he told the policeman. Brooding about the arrest of the faded blonde, Hardin put her on a train to Phoenix. She sent a telegram from Deming, New Mexico, that she was returning because she had just had a premonition that something terrible was about to happen to Hardin. The premonition troubled Hardin. Perhaps he remembered the prediction of the gypsy on the creek north of Austin.

Early in the evening of August 19, 1895, Hardin told friends that one more day would finish his book. A little later, while walking along San Antonio Street near the Acme Saloon, he saw young Selman and showered him with verbal abuse. The policeman had nerve, but he knew better than to draw against Hardin.

Later, Hardin strolled into the Acme Saloon, which had only a few customers that night. He drank a little and tried a few games. About eleven o'clock, in a good humor, he matched dice with an El Paso grocer. As he rolled the dice, he had his back to the front door.

Old John Selman walked in, drew his revolver, took careful aim, and shot Hardin in the back of the head. One of the West's most dangerous and efficient killers fell to the floor dead.

The Brushy Creek gypsy had missed one of his predictions. Hardin may have wanted to kill the Selmans, father and son, but during his seventeen months as a free man after his pardon, he had killed no one.

Hardin's life was a tragedy from a family point of view. His first wife opposed her own family to stick by him for many years. After she died and he won release from prison, he married a fifteen-year-old beauty, who left him after a few hours. His life ended in a brutal slaying brought on by his relationship with an ex-prostitute. Incidentally, Callie Lewis Hardin later married a physician and won respect from all in Mason and Kimble Counties, but she never wanted to talk about Hardin.

Family Troubles

On Sunday night, June 23, 1878, the twelve jail inmates of Shackelford County in Albany, Texas, lay down, one by one, to get some sleep. Each had leg irons on his ankles and was chained from his hand manacles to a wall of the little picket house that served as a temporary jail. Shortly after midnight Hurricane Bill Martin, chained on one side of John Larn, heard the familiar tramp, tramp of approaching vigilantes. He slid away from Larn as far as he could and turned his face to the wall, hoping no one would think he recognized them. So did the man on Larn's other side.

Larn had slept fitfully, and he, too, heard the men approach. There were nine, each wearing a long, cattleman's slicker and with a bandana covering his face below the eyes to avoid recognition. The two jail guards had quietly handed over their guns and accepted the vigilantes' suggestion to step outside and study the stars.

Larn recognized his brothers-in-law among the nine as they approached. Both had married sisters of his wife, Mary. *I wonder if Mary saw them*, he thought. He stood to face his executioners.

Across the small town square, on the second floor of Shield's Boarding House, Mary Larn had tired of her vigil and lain down beside their four-year-old son, Will. She, too, tried to get some sleep.

After the masked men stopped, their leader spoke. The men's determined eyes glinted and their raised pistols reflected faint light from the end of the hall. "In recognition of your better qualities, John Larn, we are not going to hang you," the leader said.

Lifting his chin in defiance, Larn sneered, "You're all cowards, the lot of you. Your guts stink of it."

The answering fusillade woke Mary, and her screams pierced the warm June night.

John Larn was born in Georgia about 1849. He came to Patterson's Hollow, near Rocky Ford, Colorado, in his early teens. There he killed a rancher in an argument over a horse. Shortly after, he killed a sheriff in New Mexico. By 1871, when he was twenty-two, he was a trail foreman for Bill Hayes, a stockman near Fort Griffin, Texas.

The fort had been established in Shackelford County by the army in 1867 near the southwest bank of the Clear Fork of the Brazos River. When the fort was relocated to higher ground, the area between it and the river became the town of Fort Griffin (aka the Flat) and was soon populated by some of the West's wildest and most colorful desperadoes. Very soon, the county seat moved to Albany, fifteen miles south.

The Clear Fork's largest ranchers were Joe Matthews and B. W. Reynolds. Longtime friends before they moved to the area, they became neighbors, ranching six miles east of the fort. Matthews had one son and nine daughters. Three of Reynolds' sons married Matthews girls, but the youngest Matthews girl— and some say the most beautiful—fell for John Larn at first sight. That fall of 1871 Larn drove a herd of four hundred cattle to Colorado. They rode down the Goodnight-Loving Trail to Horsehead Crossing on the Pecos River. There Larn killed two young Mexicans to get their horses. He threw their bodies into the river and returned to his herd with two good horses, saddles, and bridles.

The next day Larn discovered that they were being followed by twelve black cavalrymen. Fearing that the troopers knew they had avoided brand inspectors back on the trail, Larn and a few of the crew ambushed the soldiers and asked what they wanted.

"We're just looking for a little fresh meat to eat," their leader said, warily eyeing the drawn pistols.

Larn provided the meat, and he and the rest of the trail crew laughed at how their bluff had worked. Later on, as the herd moved north into New Mexico, Larn and his point rider killed a young Mexican sheepherder. No reason was ever given except that Larn did not like Mexicans.

Hayes met the herd about fifty miles south of Trinidad. By then it numbered 1,700 head. Hayes was pleased with the tally, remarking that the fourfold increase was due to Larn's nerve and management.

Larn returned to Texas in 1872, and news of his killings on the trail and the showdown with the cavalry reached B. W. Reynolds soon after. He had a talk with Joe Matthews, and he and both of Mary's parents tried to persuade her to postpone the wedding planned for November.

Mary Matthews, a very pretty girl, had curly brown hair, large blue eyes, and a lovely figure. She also had a strong will. John Larn was a handsome man with broad shoulders; thick black hair; high cheekbones; dark, intelligent eyes; an aristocratic nose; and a trim mustache above a wide mouth. He did not smoke, drink, or swear in the presence of ladies. He already had a reputation in Fort Griffin as a leader of men and a charmer of women. He had abundant courage and was a superb marksman. The wedding went ahead as planned.

Larn and Mary began ranching in Throckmorton County at Camp Cooper on the northeast bank of the Clear Fork, a few miles upstream from Fort Griffin. The camp had once been commanded by Lt. Colonel Robert E. Lee, who always called it "My Texas Home." After the Civil War it served as an operational base for Ranald McKenzie's Fourth Cavalry and was abandoned by the army shortly before John and Mary settled there. Larn built a three-room stone house on the camp's parade ground (later called the "The Honeymoon Cottage"). He added stone borders for four flower beds, laying out two designs each in hearts and diamonds. Three years later he built a large, stone six-room house across the river. He located it on higher ground with cooling breezes and a commanding view. It had elegant windows with beveled glass, towering chimneys, a high-pitched roof, and a square cupola, or widow's walk. People began wondering where the money came from.

Mary's first baby, Will, was born in December 1873. Another son, Joseph, born in March 1875, died at six months of age. His parents buried him near their just-built larger house in a sixteen-foot-square plot enclosed with a stone wall.

By 1876 Larn had become a leader in the Fort Griffin Vigilance Committee and had won enough community respect to run for Shackelford County sheriff. He won, becoming the second sheriff in the county's history. By the time of his swearing-in on April 18, he had rounded up a bunch of prostitutes and bad men from the Fort Griffin Flat and had flushed out a gang of cow thieves. John Selman became his unofficial deputy and helped Larn run the rustlers off.

Selman had been a ranch hand, well respected by the Matthews and Reynolds families. He had come to the Clear Fork country in 1864 as an army deserter, bringing his widowed mother, brother, and two sisters. He was married by the time his mother died, and he moved to New Mexico and was in Dodge City, Kansas, shortly before returning to Fort Griffin. He posted bail in Dodge City for his friend Hurricane Bill Martin, a gunman with a trail of crime as far north as the Black Hills of Dakota Territory. Martin, arrested for assault to commit murder, jumped bail and showed up in Fort Griffin, where he took up with a prostitute who came to be called Hurricane Minnie.

Later events suggested that Sheriff Larn's interest in flushing out the cattle thieves had more to do with eliminating competition than enforcing the law. The ranchers in the area, including some of Larn's in-laws, began wondering if there was some connection between their losses of cattle and the obvious increase of the new sheriff's herd. Mary's dowry had included several hundred head of cattle, but the herd seemed bigger than one would expect from natural increase. Once, John Irwin saw Larn driving a bunch of cattle that weren't his, and Larn offered him $100 to keep quiet. Irwin talked, and then some remembered that two years before, a man named Bryant had lived in Larn's home and ran a few cattle with his herd. One of Larn's ranch hands killed Bryant, who had no friends or relatives with enough nerve to investigate. Larn had kept the cattle and considered the matter closed. There was talk, but Joe Matthews stood by his son-in-law, and the differences seemed settled, at least temporarily.

Until spring 1877, Larn continued to draw some support from both sides of the law. Residents of the Flat appreciated that he had chased the bad element out, but Larn's enemies in

18

the vigilantes, whom he had ridden with at one time, considered him a better target for killing while he wore the sheriff's badge. Larn not only had a quick draw, he was a good shot and he understood the outlaw mind.

In spite of Larn's attitude toward other ranchers, Mexicans, and the public in general, his life with Mary was exemplary. He was devoted to her and she to him. The community recognized him as a "kind, considerate, and loving husband."

By September 1876, Larn and Selman were spending a lot of time with a cow outfit that worked for the Millet Brothers who had ranching interests from south Texas to the Dakotas and Idaho. The crew decided to winter on the Clear Fork, about five miles west of Larn's ranch. The Millet crew was a hard-drinking, hard-riding outfit, and neighboring ranchers noticed their cattle losses increasing.

That winter Larn and Selman added some cattle to their own herd, saying they had bought the animals from two brothers who had driven them down from Indian Territory. Then rumors started that they had killed the brothers and thrown their bodies into what was called the Bottomless Wells on Tecumseh Creek. By then Selman had settled on Tecumseh Creek about four miles northeast of Camp Cooper. One of the brother's bodies surfaced, revealing that a rock had been tied to it.

On January 17, 1877, a shoot-out in the Beehive, a combination saloon, dance hall, and gambling den in the Flat, left Billy Bland, formerly the Millet Brothers' trail boss and now one of Larn's ranch hands, dead. Also killed were two innocent bystanders—a popular young lawyer, recently married, and a cavalry officer, recently discharged. Larn's principal deputy,

John Larn's grave near Fort Griffin, Texas. *Author's photo collection*

William Cruger, and County Attorney William Jeffries were wounded but recovered.

The fight had started when Bland and another Larn ranch hand, both drunk, had galloped into town, yelling and firing their six-shooters.

Larn immediately resigned, protesting that Bland's killing by his deputy Cruger was unprovoked. Cruger took his place. Rumors about rustling continued until Larn and his ranch hands began leaving the ranch headquarters at night to sleep up in the hills. This led to some kind of truce between the vigilantes and Larn, under which Larn and Selman were appointed Deputy Inspectors of Hides and Animals for Shackelford County in April 1877.

The new deputies had several duties. They had to inspect all cattle herds entering or leaving the county. Fort Griffin was on the Western Cattle Trail, a popular route for moving beef to the railheads in Kansas. A questionable trail herd could be passed if money was paid under the saddle horn, and such reports eventually surfaced about Larn and Selman.

Butchers in the county had to make regular reports of the beeves butchered and show the hides as proof. The two new deputy hide inspectors contracted to furnish beef to the army post at Fort Griffin. Selman knew the butcher trade, and he and Larn were the men responsible for inspecting the hides. The opportunity was too good to pass up. With a guaranteed market for the beef and no one to ask them about the hides, which could be hidden in the river, rustling was guaranteed to be profitable. Their bonds for the inspector position were signed by Joe Matthews, Larn's father-in-law, and by Frank E. Conrad, the best-known merchant on the

Texas frontier, who would later marry another Matthews daughter.

In February 1878, Texas Rangers found six beef hides hidden in the Clear Fork of the Brazos near Larn's slaughter pens. None of the brands were his. No one knows why the Rangers didn't search for more hides. There were rumors that Larn, Selman, and Hurricane Bill Martin had agreed to cooperate with the Rangers who had been investigating vigilante hangings. All three had been vigilantes and knew who the others were. Some of the rancher vigilantes got Judge J. R. Fleming—who had also been a member—to request that the governor disband the Rangers' investigation. That was done, but fear that one or more of the trio had revealed names still pervaded the community.

Hurricane Bill was particularly bitter at the vigilante committee. Earlier he usually had been the man they paid to cut the victims down after a hanging. Yet committee members had once forced him to marry Hurricane Minnie and then nearly hanged him for going through with the ceremony. The bitterness never left.

Another rumor that appeared in spring 1877 was that Larn had hired two brothers named Williams to build a rock wall a mile and a half long near his house. Instead of paying, he shot the men and threw their bodies in the Clear Fork. A body was found but could not be identified. Feeling in the community divided sharply about this rumor. Larn's brothers-in-law, who thought him guilty of rustling, refused to believe that he would kill a workman to avoid paying for the labor.

In early June 1878, someone shot a farmer named Lancaster who had furnished the information that led to the dragging of the river and the discovery of two hundred hides with local brands. Lancaster swore to the sheriff that Larn and Selman had chased him along the Clear Fork bank and shot him. He hid in the brush until they were gone.

A week later Larn ambushed a well-known rancher named Treadwell. He made a long rifle shot and missed Treadwell but killed his horse.

By now Larn and Selman were in open war against everyone. Some ranchers went to Joe Matthews and asked him to do something about his son-in-law. Matthews talked to Larn but got nowhere. He threw up his hands in despair and told his neighbors he could do no more.

The civil authorities who had turned a deaf ear to the men's escapades while they were fellow vigilantes now decided to hunt them down. Farmer Lancaster, in spite of having been shot at, had the courage to swear out warrants against Larn and Selman. Sheriff Cruger picked his men carefully. They included George and Ben Reynolds, each married to a sister of Mary. Others included a deputy sheriff, a former city marshal of Fort Griffin, and the rancher Treadwell.

Hurricane Minnie learned about the planned arrests. She got a horse and rode out to warn both men. She missed Larn's house in the dark but did warn Selman. He grabbed a rifle and rode four miles to Larn's place, either to warn him or to help him resist the posse. He got there just in time to observe from a high bluff that the posse was already there. He escaped.

A second posse, including another of Larn's brothers-in-law, had left Albany to arrest Selman, who was gone when the posse arrived.

Larn had walked down to his cow pens to milk when Cruger's posse arrived. Just as he sat down on the milking stool,

Cruger and Ben Reynolds stepped up, their guns drawn. Larn handed over his pistol saying, "I saw some men near the house a while back, but I thought they were Rangers. I wasn't expecting trouble."

"There'll be no trouble if you stay peaceable, John."

In fact the posses had been kept secret from the Rangers, who knew nothing about the attempts to arrest Larn and Selman.

Larn thought he was going to Fort Griffin, where friends from the Flat could be counted on to help free him. When Sheriff Cruger said the warrant was from Albany, he knew he was in serious trouble.

"Could I go in to say goodbye to Mary?" he asked. He hoped to get another gun and fight his way out.

"You can't go back in the house."

Seeing no Rangers in the posse, Larn feared that he would be hanged before he got to Albany. "Could you at least bring Mary and the boy out so they can go to town with us?"

Mary's brothers-in-law didn't know how to refuse that request.

On the way through Fort Griffin Mary left the group to talk to John W. Wray, a newly arrived lawyer and about the only one in the county with no association with the vigilantes. "I'll be on to Albany as soon as possible," she told her husband. "I'll get a room in Shields' for Will and me if we don't have you out by dark."

Larn looked at his wife and son and nodded glumly.

When the posse reached Albany, they stopped at a blacksmith shop where Charley Reinbold riveted leg irons and fastened them to Larn. His hands had already been manacled. Then, clamping along with the whole town watching, he entered the jail and was chained to a wall with the twelve other prisoners.

When Mary brought John W. Wray to Albany, the lawyer tried unsuccessfully to get Justice of the Peace Edgar Rye to release Larn on bond. In his book *The Quirt and the Spur*, Rye admitted that Wray warned him that his client's life was in danger from vigilantes. Rye felt that Selman's gang would attempt a rescue, and he would not interfere with the sheriff's arrangements to hold the prisoner, as he had already doubled the guard and had ten men in reserve.

"Well, your honor," Wray pleaded, "if Larn is killed during the night, I will not be responsible for it; I have tried to do my duty."

"No one can censure you for being true to your client, Wray," Rye said. "And I am also conscious of performing my duty as a state officer."

At ten o'clock that night, Deputy City Marshal of Fort Griffin, John Poe, relieved R. A. Slack, who was guarding the prisoners. Slack went to sleep in a small side room. Two hours later he was awakened with a pistol poking into his ribs. He jumped up, but nine masked men surrounded him and grabbed his arms. Poe had also been overpowered, but he had been a vigilante, and he may not have tried very hard to protect his prisoner.

In fairness to Poe, he eventually came to believe more in law than in vigilantism. His change of mind may have occurred at this time. Three years later, Poe, then a deputy in New Mexico, would be present when Sheriff Pat Garrett killed Billy the Kid.

The day after the shooting, Mary Larn took her husband's body home to be buried in the backyard of their home, near their second child. Stone walls in a sixteen-foot square still surround the little graveyard.

Death Dances
on the Border

Arkansas-born John Selman was five feet, ten inches tall and lean. His eyes—so light in color that one could hardly tell where the white ended and the blue began—gave his face a strange, unearthly appearance. Strangers would pay him little note.

Selman had been a sharpshooter in the Confederate Army, but he walked away twice from his duties. The first time he returned, absent without leave; the second time, he deserted.

Frank Collinson, rancher, buffalo hunter, and author, knew Selman, John Wesley Hardin, and George Scarborough personally. He described how Sheriff John Larn and Selman, his deputy, took care of troublemakers at Fort Griffin in the fall of 1875. Once, Larn and Selman confronted a buffalo skinner from Bitter Creek who had been painting up the town.

"Throw up your hands," Larn demanded.

Collinson continued: "The badman reached back for his gun and Selman shot him that second. The wounded man kind of reached over, put his hands on the ground, and Selman stuck his pistol close to his ear and gave him the mercy shot. They got an old goods box, put him in, got a man to dig a hole behind the dance hall, and dumped him in this hole. The transaction did not take more than an hour. That was a fair sample of how they ran a tough town."

The night the vigilantes in Albany came for Larn, Hurricane Minnie, a former prostitute and now wife of Hurricane Bill, warned Selman and tried unsuccessfully to warn Larn. By the time Minnie knew that she was too late to warn Larn, Selman and younger brother Tom were riding fast for New Mexico. Selman and Minnie had their own intimate relationship while Hurricane Bill was in jail with Hardin. Selman left his pregnant wife and their four children behind when he fled, and his wife died in childbirth.

By summer 1878, both Selmans were involved in the Lincoln County War in New Mexico. John kept to the fringes of that war, and no one knows how many he killed. He did kill another man in a dispute over gang leadership, and the next six months saw six men killed by the gang.

After almost perishing from smallpox in Mexico, John Selman showed up in the Fort Davis–Fort Stockton area of West Texas. By this time Nicanora, a Mexican woman who nursed him through smallpox, was traveling with him as his wife. The Rangers arrested both Selmans in August 1880, and took them back to Shackelford County for trial on charges of cattle rustling. Vigilantes lynched Tom, and the Shackelford officials didn't want to hold John's trial, so they let him escape.

Eventually, while living in Mexico, Selman and Nicanora obtained custody of two of Selman's children. Nicanora had been a schoolteacher and was a devout Catholic and a charming lady. She and her father, a traveling tailor, had discovered Selman near death from smallpox when they saw a line of buzzards, waiting in the desert. Selman, starving and raving from thirst, was covered with blowflies. Maggots had crawled into scratches on his bloody legs. Nicanora cleaned him up, dug out the maggots, and nursed him back to life. Selman had a gold-filled money belt around his waist. He offered it to Nicanora and her father. They refused the offer, and he always had a warm spot in his heart for Mexicans afterward.

Selman operated a saloon in the state of Chihuahua, went broke, did some mining, and borrowed $25 from his son to buy into a poker game where he won another saloon and $800. He returned to El Paso in 1888 after he learned that the old cattle-rustling charges in Albany had finally been dismissed.

El Paso, Texas's most western town, occupied a narrow strip of land squeezed between Mexico on the south and New Mexico Territory of the United States on the north. It was full of rough, quick-shooting men, some of whom worked for the law while many others ran from it.

At first no one paid much attention to Selman. Then, in November 1891, he was savagely attacked by two men and almost killed. There was speculation that he knew his attackers, but he refused to say anything about it. The mystery was never solved. A year later Selman became a constable in El Paso. Apparently Nicanora had died by then.

Selman, almost fifty-four, married sixteen-year-old Romula Granadino on August 23, 1893. The next day's newspaper said that "although he had been younger, he had never looked handsomer or happier."

But this marriage was stormy. Selman's two sons, who now had a stepmother younger than they, did not approve, and they moved out. Most of Selman's work now involved arresting petty offenders, but on April 5, 1894, he ran into Bass Outlaw (his real name), a former Texas Ranger who had become a terror when drunk. Outlaw was chasing a brothel operator, Tillie

Howard, down the street when another Texas Ranger objected. Outlaw shot the man Ranger to death. When Selman intervened, Outlaw fired a bullet so close to Selman's face that the powder seared his eyes, almost blinding him. Reeling backward and firing by instinct, the old constable dropped the ex-Ranger with a shot just above the heart. Outlaw fired twice more before he fell, hitting Selman twice in the legs.

Selman used a cane the rest of his life and never recovered his full vision. Outlaw died, and for some strange reason Selman was charged with his murder. At the trial, the judge instructed the jury to find Selman not guilty.

By fall 1894, Jeff Milton had been hired as city marshal of El Paso. The man who was born while his father—a descendant of England's great epic poet—was governor of Florida soon appointed Selman's son John Junior to the El Paso police force, giving him the same beat as his father. The next summer El Paso citizens had had enough of Milton's attempt to clean up their town. They elected a new mayor who promptly appointed to the office of city marshal a man whom Milton had previously fired from the police force. Milton then became a deputy United States marshal, serving with another deputy, George Scarborough. The elder Selman and Scarborough became close friends. Scarborough had at one time been sheriff of Jones County, Texas.

By this time John Wesley Hardin was in El Paso, and the stage was set for a bewildering series of events. Only the trigger was needed, and one of the West's strangest cowboys—called Martin Morose—filled the role.

A big, blond, coarse native of Poland, his name was probably something like Mroz. He disdained to wear underwear and he wore heavy clodhopper work shoes instead of boots, but he knew the value of a cow. Morose had ridden a stolen horse from Helena, a Polish settlement in south Texas, to Eddy (present-day Carlsbad), New Mexico. He didn't wait to raise his own cattle; he rustled from others. He found his entertainment in El Paso, and he married Helen Billyoh, formerly employed at Billie Howard's brothel.

When the law got interested in Morose in New Mexico, he fled to Old Mexico to escape arrest. Poor Helen, by then somewhat the worse for wear but still slender with forty-year-old good looks and a five-year-old son, employed Hardin as her lawyer. She thought she wanted Morose back in El Paso with protection from the law, but her interest in her Polish cowboy was soon replaced by her interest in her new lawyer.

In the meantime, Jeff Milton and George Scarborough developed an interest in the reward that had been offered for Morose. They decided to entice Morose to cross into Texas where they could arrest him and turn him over to New Mexico authorities for the reward.

On June 21, 1895, Scarborough escorted Morose across the international border, where Milton and Texas Ranger Frank McMahon, Scarborough's brother-in-law, were waiting. A wild barrage of gunfire broke out, and when it ended, Morose had fallen with eight pistol bullets and two shotgun slugs in his body. Scarborough was usually credited with the killing.

El Paso citizens were shocked—it wasn't that they liked Morose, but they thought the officers had not played fair. Scarborough, Milton, and McMahon were all charged with murder, and all acquitted in separate trials. The only mourners at Morose's funeral were his wife and her current bed companion, John Wesley Hardin.

In August 1895, John Selman Jr. disarmed a very drunk Helen Morose, and she paid a fine for carrying a concealed weapon. Hardin was away in Pecos at the time. When he returned to town a few days later, Hardin berated both Selmans and bragged that he would kill them for the insult to Helen.

When old John Selman heard that Hardin was on the prod for him, he took matters into his own hands. At 11 p.m. on July 19, 1895, Selman walked into the Acme Saloon and saw Hardin rolling dice at the bar. Hardin had just called out "four sixes to beat," when Selman fired a bullet that took off the back of Hardin's head. Taking no chances, Selman pumped two more bullets into Hardin's body as it lay on the floor. Young John Selman ran into the saloon, grabbed his father, and shouted, "Don't shoot any more, Pa; he's dead!"

Selman claimed that Hardin had moved for his gun, but no witness supported him. Selman employed lawyer Albert Fall—later the central figure in the Teapot Dome Scandal—to defend him. Fall argued to the jury that his client, whose vision was clearly impaired, had seen Hardin in the saloon mirror and thought the man was facing him and drawing his gun. Enough doubt was raised that the jury acquitted the killer of Texas's most renowned killer.

A few months later Selman accused his friend George Scarborough of stealing money from Morose's corpse after the assassination on the international border. Both men brooded about their falling out. At 4 a.m. on April 6, 1896, Selman was drinking in El Paso's Wigwam Saloon when Scarborough walked in.

"Come outside, I want to talk to you," Selman said. They walked to an alley beside the saloon.

Selman's son was in a Juarez jail. "I want you to go over the river with me this morning," Selman said. "We must get that boy out of jail."

"I'll go," Scarborough said. "But I won't stand for any funny business in Juarez."

Selman squinted at him as he swayed on his feet.

"Come to think about it," Scarborough continued, "I reckon I'll just kill you now."

He shot his old friend three times and ran. When the police arrived, Selman was barely alive. His holster was empty.

"Who shot you?" the police asked their old partner from days gone by.

"That sonofabitch Scarborough."

"What happened to your gun?"

"Somebody stole it 'fore you got here."

Scarborough was found not guilty of murdering his former friend, but he resigned as deputy marshal. On April 5, 1900, while working as a privately employed livestock detective in the Chiricahua Mountains of Arizona, Scarborough and another man were riding in close pursuit of a remnant of the Butch Cassidy Wild Bunch gang. Suddenly a .30-40 bullet slammed through his leg, killing his horse. He was taken by wagon and railroad to Deming, New Mexico, where his leg was amputated.

George Scarborough died the next day, four years to the day after he had killed John Selman. The bizarre dance of death that had started five years before had finally come to an end.

Born to Hang

A fair description of John Wesley Hardin would be a juvenile punk who enjoyed killing blacks, Yankee soldiers, Mexicans, and Indians. Jim Miller, Hardin's cousin by marriage, is seldom mentioned in Texas history, but a fair description of him is worse. He killed his grandparents when he was eight and his brother-in-law when he was seventeen. Eventually he preyed on the world at large, demanding money for his services.

Miller, a slender five feet, ten inches tall and a dapper dresser, never swore, drank, or smoked. He had many friends and attended church so regularly that he was often called "Deacon Jim." He was usually soft-spoken, but his pale-blue cold, unblinking eyes gave some people goose bumps. When he killed his sister's husband John Coop on Sunday, July 30, 1884, he left during an evening worship service and galloped three miles to Coop's house, where his victim was sleeping on an outside porch. Miller crept up and shot Coop in the head and rode back to the church before the service ended. Despite his alibi about being in church at the time, the jury convicted him, and the judge gave him life in prison. But Miller appealed and got a new trial and an acquittal. The bizarre crime and its bizarre result became typical of Texas's leading assassin.

Miller was born in Van Buren, Arkansas, in 1866, one of nine children. His parents moved to Franklin, Robertson County, Texas, when Miller was a baby. When they died, he was sent to live with his grandparents in Coryell County. There was no other suspect for their murder in their own home, and Miller was arrested but released as too young to prosecute. Turned over to the custody of his sister, he soon clashed with her husband on their farm at nearby Gatesville.

Three years after Miller killed his brother-in-law he got a cowboy job with Mannen Clements, Hardin's cousin. He married Mannen's daughter, Sally, in February 1888, exactly twelve months after Sally's father had been killed by Ballinger City Marshal Joseph Townsend over a political dispute. Miller later avenged this killing by blasting Townsend out of his saddle from ambush as the marshal rode home one night.

Miller spent the next two years drifting around southeastern New Mexico Territory. Sometimes he gambled in saloons on the Mexican border; sometimes he rode into west Texas towns. One August afternoon in 1891 he rode into Pecos, seat of Reeves County. Oppressive heat hung heavy above the baked streets, and bystanders wondered why the stranger wore a black broadcloth coat.

Miller swung down in front of Juan's Saloon, and curious heads appeared in windows and doorways to watch. A half dozen cowboys from a rough cow outfit near Toyah and their ramrod, a man named Hearn, studied Miller carefully as he entered the saloon. After Miller ordered a glass of water, Hearn stepped up to the bar next to him.

"That big coat of yours sure makes me sweat," Hearn sneered. His cowboys felt duty bound to challenge someone every time they came to town.

Miller's eyes never changed, but his nose wrinkled in disgust at the dust-covered men with cow dung on their boots. "Your stink makes me sick," he said.

"Take it off," Hearn ordered, pointing with his left hand at Miller's coat.

Hearn's right hand moved too fast to see, and he had it on the butt of his revolver when Miller's revolver seemed to leap from under his coat into his hand, its muzzle against Hearn's belly.

"Drop it," Miller said softly. The room was suddenly silent.

Hearn's half-drawn six-shooter slid back into its holster. "Hell's bells," he muttered, his face suddenly ashen. "I was just a foolin'."

Miller stepped back, never taking his cold eyes off Hearn. "I like this town and figure to settle here. You have two minutes to get out, and take these jackasses with you." He nodded at the other cowboys. "If you come back to raise more hell, I'll kill you."

When the dust of the departing cowboys had settled, Miller bought drinks for his wide-eyed audience and had another glass of water. The story swept through the small town, and its saloon soon filled. Even Sheriff Bud Frazer came in to order a round of drinks.

Other people had declined to ask about the coat, but Frazer inquired, "Would you mind telling me, sir, why you wear such a heavy coat in weather like this?"

The crowd tensed, but Miller smiled softly. "This coat is my life insurance. It belonged to an old friend of mine. He sheriffed on the border for years and never got a scratch." The crowd relaxed, and Miller continued. "He gave credit to the coat, and he died in bed with his boots off." Miller stroked his worn coat. "He gave it to me. I figured it must be lucky."

"Well, a man's got a right to his own superstition," the sheriff said. "You say you're going to settle down here?"

"Thought I'd see about working in a hotel. I've done some of that."

"Let's go down to my office. I'd like to propose something you might be interested in."

Miller left the sheriff's office wearing a deputy's badge. Without knowing it, Frazer had deputized Texas's first hired assassin. He would soon become the most dangerous man in Texas, New Mexico, and Oklahoma.

Frazer and Miller worked well together and seemed to like each other. Then suddenly they had a falling out, and no one knew why. Some thought Frazer had stumbled onto evidence that Miller was running stolen cattle into Mexico. At any rate, Con Gibson told Frazer that Miller and Mannen Clements had tried to get him to help them kill Frazer. Then a Ranger captain came to town and arrested Miller.

Miller hired two fine lawyers (one would later be a district judge and the other a state senator), and he got an easy acquittal.

Con Gibson, the informer on Miller, left town in a hurry. When he reached Carlsbad, New Mexico, he got into an argument with John Denston, a cousin of Miller's wife. The argument ended with Gibson's funeral, and people considered it a revenge killing, but nothing implicated Miller. Only Bud Frazer seemed to be bitter.

On April 12, 1894, Miller, still wearing his frock coat, was talking to a rancher friend who noticed that Bud Frazer kept walking back and forth near them. Miller, engrossed in the conversation, hadn't noticed.

"I wonder why the sheriff keeps walking by and looking at your back," the friend said.

"Well, I don't know." Miller turned around and stared into the muzzle of the sheriff's six-shooter.

"Jim, you're a cattle rustler and a murderer," Frazer shouted, opening fire. "Here's one for Con Gibson."

Frazer's gun roared, and the first bullet ricocheted off Miller's coat.

Frazer's second shot disabled Miller's gun arm. Miller got his pistol into his left hand and blazed away, but Frazer escaped unhit.

Frazer emptied his gun, but Miller stayed on his feet and kept shooting. When Miller finally fell, Frazer went back to his office, unhurt. By all rights, Deacon Jim Miller should have been dead.

The people who picked Miller up and carried him to his hotel discovered that three of Frazer's bullets had struck directly over Miller's heart. They had flattened against the steel plate he wore over his chest and under his coat. Then, for the first time, Miller's own friends learned why he wore that black coat even in the heat of summer.

When Miller regained consciousness, he smiled at his friends and said, "Tell Frazer he can't kill me, and he can't run me out. Next time, I'll get him."

Miller took several months getting well, but he repeated his oath that he would kill Frazer if he had to crawl twenty miles on his knees to do it. In the meantime Frazer lost an election and moved to Lordsburg, New Mexico, to visit relatives.

Unfortunately Frazer returned in December. He rode into Pecos the day after Christmas and saw Miller standing in front

Multiple hangings in stable at Ada, Oklahoma, on April 19, 1909. Jim Miller is on the left. *Research Division of the Oklahoma Historical Society, Tom Brett Collection*

of the blacksmith shop. Knowing of Miller's oath to kill him, Frazer drew his revolver and began shooting. His first bullet hit Miller's gun arm and the second hit his leg. Then he aimed for the heart. Miller, although again disabled, fired away with his left hand. Frazer again shot Miller over the heart and wondered why the man was still standing. He had never heard about the steel breastplate. Knowing that he was a good shot, the confused attacker turned and fled.

Miller's friends wanted to go after Frazer, but he smiled and said he'd try the legal way first. He swore out a complaint with the new sheriff.

Frazer's trial was moved to El Paso, and Miller hired his cousin, John Wesley Hardin, to assist in the prosecution. But Hardin was killed before it came to trial, and the jury disagreed. The trial was moved to Colorado City in Mitchell County, and Frazer won an acquittal in May 1896.

Miller, disgusted, determined to get Frazer once and for all. It took four months of waiting, while spies from each side reported on the other's movements, but Miller finally heard in September that Frazer was visiting relatives in Toyah, a tiny town eighteen miles from Pecos.

Knowing that Frazer would be advised of his every step, Miller got a friend, Bill Earhart, to wait outside Pecos with two horses. Then he sauntered out of town on foot to meet Earhart and the two rode to Toyah. Earhart rented a hotel room across the street from the saloon on the night of September 13, and Miller slipped into the room by the back way.

The next morning, Frazer went to the saloon as usual and started playing cards with friends. Earhart signaled that all was clear, and Miller walked rapidly across the street with his shotgun. He pushed the swinging door open and fired both barrels. The double-barreled charge practically blew Frazer's head from his body.

One witness reported: "All of a sudden the room exploded like dynamite had hit the floor. I happened to be looking at Bud, and like to have fainted when I saw his whole head disappear in a clot of splashing blood and bone. That's all I took time to see. I dived through the window, taking glass and all with me. Next thing I remember I was under my bed three blocks away, shivering like hell."

Frazer's sister borrowed a gun and, with her mother, set out for Pecos. She confronted Miller when he arrived, covering him with the pistol.

"If you try to use that gun," Miller said softly, "I'll give you what your brother got. I'll shoot you right in the face."

She lowered the gun but gave Miller a vicious tongue-lashing. One of Frazer's friends, Barney Riggs, caught up with Earhart and killed him along with another of Miller's friends.

Miller's trial for murdering Frazer was transferred to Eastland, between Abilene and Fort Worth. Miller moved to Eastland well in advance of trial, went into business as a hotel operator, transferred his church membership, contributed to local charities, and did everything he could to make a good impression. Also, he had his wife and two sons—five and two years old—with him.

The three-week trial started in June 1897. Dozens of people came from Pecos to testify. One said Miller's conduct was as "exemplary as that of a minister of the gospel." Nevertheless, eleven jurors voted to convict. The one holdout made a second trial necessary. At the second trial Miller was acquitted on grounds of self-defense.

After keeping a saloon in Memphis in the Texas Panhandle, and even working for a time as a Texas Ranger, Miller went to Monahans, back in the Pecos area, where he apparently became a deputy United States marshal. For the next eight years he killed sheepmen and farmers, both classes despised by some West Texas ranchers. His standard price was $150 per man. Once Miller said with pride, "I have killed eleven men that I know about; I've lost my notch stick on sheepherders I've killed out on the border."

In February 1908, Miller killed Pat Garrett, the legendary lawman who had killed Billy the Kid. Sheriff Garrett had killed the famous outlaw over twenty-five years before. The controversy over the killing—Garrett and Billy the Kid had been friends, and Garrett shot him without warning in a darkened room—made Garrett lose the next election, and he took up ranching. For the next twenty years Garrett ranched, served as a captain in the Texas Rangers, again as a New Mexico sheriff, and as a collector of customs appointed by President Theodore Roosevelt. For five years he raised racehorses in Uvalde, Texas, where John Garner, a young friend of his, would later become vice president of the United States.

By 1906 Garrett had a little ranch in the Organ Mountains east of Las Cruces, New Mexico. The land was coveted by W. W. Cox, a neighboring rancher, who could not get Garrett to sell. Somebody hired Miller to kill Garrett so Cox could get the land. Miller's price for this killing was $1,500.

Garrett was shot in the back of the head on February 29, 1908. He had been traveling toward Las Cruces in a buggy, accompanied by Carl Adamson. Wayne Brazil joined them on the way on horseback. Five miles from Las Cruces, the buggy stopped, and while Garrett was urinating someone shot him in the back of the head. He fell to the ground, dead, and he was shot again in the stomach. Brazil and Adamson went on to Las Cruces, where Brazil turned himself in to the sheriff, saying he had shot Garrett in self-defense. Adamson backed up his story.

Captain Fred Fornoff of the Territorial Mounted Police investigated the murder scene after the sheriff picked up the body. He found where a horse and rider had waited nearby for some time, leaving two .44 Winchester spent cartridges in the sand.

At a farce of a trial in which the jury heard only Brazil's story of shooting in self-defense—Garrett's heavy driving glove was still on his right (gun) hand and his fly was open—the jury acquitted Brazil. Captain Fornoff was never produced as a witness.

With the proof that the horse that waited beside the trail had been borrowed by Jim Miller and that the bullet that entered the back of Garrett's head came from his rifle, it is not surprising that most historians agree that Miller killed Garrett.

Miller spent the rest of 1908 back in Fort Worth gambling. Late that year he heard that his old friend Mannie Clements had been killed. He swore he would avenge the killing, but he had already been hired for another job, this time in Oklahoma. The fee was the highest he had ever been offered—$2,000.

Ada, Oklahoma, the scene of Miller's last killing and his own death, had a little over three thousand people and thirty-six murders in 1908. Gunfighters from two powerful factions had been feuding for years. Angus Bobbitt led one faction; Joe Allen and Jesse West led the other. Finally, Bobbitt forced Allen and West out. They moved their cattle herds to Hemphill County, Texas, and brooded like wounded rattlesnakes. The killing of Pat Garrett hastened their decision on how to strike back.

In late February 1909, a frock-coated man was seen riding near Bobbitt's home a few miles from Ada. In late afternoon on February 27, Bobbitt was driving home with a wagonload of meal cake for his cattle. A neighbor, Bob Ferguson, followed in his own wagon. Just before sundown, they met a lone rider who talked a few minutes with Bobbitt and then rode on, passing out of view as he crossed over a hill behind them.

Just after sundown, about a mile from Bobbitt's ranch, a double-barreled shotgun sounded twice. Bobbitt, struck twice, toppled from his wagon, dead. Ferguson recognized the man they had met earlier on the trail as he galloped away.

The sheriff followed the killer's tracks to the farm of young John Williamson. The shoes worn by the mare Williamson had rented had been removed, but were found under the kitchen floor. Williamson withstood a lot of pressure before he identified the rider who had rented his horse as his uncle from Fort Worth, Jim Miller. More investigation revealed that Berry Burrell, an old friend of Allen and West, was intermediary between them and Miller and had spotted Bobbitt for the killer. Miller was arrested on March 30 near Fort Worth. Burrell had already been arrested in Fort Worth. Afraid that Allen and West would fight extradition, the county attorney sent them this telegram at Canadian, Texas: "You and Joe come to Ada at once. Need $10,000, Miller."

The ruse worked, and Allen and West were arrested in Oklahoma City, just after stepping off the train to be greeted by their lawyer. The preliminary hearing was held on March 19. Some of Ada's citizens didn't wait for the trial.

At two o'clock in the morning of April 19, a group of vigilantes cut off Ada's electric current. In the darkness they overpowered the jailers and removed Miller, Allen, West, and Burrell. They took them to a livery stable and hanged all four. They saved Jim Miller for last. He refused to confess, merely saying, "Just let the record show that I've killed fifty-one men."

Miller was as unconcerned about his own death as he had been earlier about each of his many victims. The vigilantes stood him on a box, adjusted the noose around his neck, and told him to step forward to the edge of the box. Miller slipped a diamond ring from his hand, directing that it be given to his wife. He made other dispositions of his property.

"I'd like to have my coat," he said. "I don't want to die naked." He must have believed it would still make him invincible.

They refused, so he asked for his hat. They jammed his Stetson on his head.

Miller laughed. "Now I'm ready. I don't want this rope to knock my hat off. You sure you got it set right?"

The vigilantes looked on with amazement as they nodded their heads.

"I always knew I was born to hang," Miller continued. "They never was a bullet that could kill me."

He moved forward to the edge of the box. He looked down and laughed again.

"Let 'er rip," he shouted as he leaped forward.

Some people said Miller's conduct on the box showed his courage. Others said it showed his total depravity and inhumanity.

One of the vigilantes draped Miller's coat over his slumped shoulders as he hung there in the barn. "It won't do him no good, now," he said.

A Foolish Boast

Texas's most unusual outlaw was a forty-eight-year-old Kiowa Indian chief. Found guilty of murder by a jury in the state's most sensational—and probably weirdest—trial, he was sentenced to death. This was the first—and apparently only—time an Indian chief was prosecuted in an American criminal court. He won a commutation from the governor and a later release from custody only to be returned to prison. The renowned warrior, orator, and diplomat tried to understand the invaders who had taken away his people's land and treated him so strangely in court, but, dispirited with the return to prison, he committed suicide.

Satanta (White Bear), a bold, broad-shouldered man over six feet tall, had always sought power among his people. Jovial with friends and merciless with enemies, a man of great vitality with a commanding presence, Satanta had been a warrior chief for three decades when he rode with other chiefs and a hundred warriors out of their Fort Sill Reservation to cross the Red River into Texas on May 15, 1871. In the rear rode seventy-year-old Satank, the head chief of the nation. Big Tree, Satanta's cousin and already a war chief at twenty-two, rode near the front, eager to count coup and add to his growing laurels.

Satanta had impressed the whites four years before at Medicine Lodge, Kansas, where seven thousand Indians from five southern plains tribes had gathered to make a peace treaty. Fluent in five languages, he spoke for all the assembled tribes, and the whites called him the Orator of the Plains. Neither the government nor the Indians had kept their treaty obligations.

45

Raids continued, and now old Satank grieved the loss of his oldest son on a raid into Texas just one year before.

The second day after crossing the Red River the Indians entered Young County and headed for the Butterfield Trail where they hoped to surprise traders who were traveling alone or in small groups. Owl Prophet, a warrior chief as well as a medicine man, consulted his oracle and reported that the next day two parties of whites would pass over the road.

"The first will be small," Owl Prophet said. "But the medicine is not right to attack it. We must wait for the second party. That attack will succeed."

At daybreak on May 18 the Indians took a position commanding a long stretch of the road as it crossed Salt Creek Prairie. Close to noon, a single army wagon behind a small mounted escort came into view from the west. Younger warriors yearned to attack, but Owl Prophet insisted on waiting for the second party. They did not know that the four passengers in the wagon were two colonels and a brigadier general and the man they served as aides, William T. Sherman, commanding general of the United States Army. Of course the soldiers were unaware that a hundred pairs of hostile eyes had watched them pass.

About three hours later a wagon train came into view from the east. The younger warriors stopped complaining about Owl Prophet's decision. Now they could ride against the enemy! Satanta carried a bugle that he had captured from soldiers and enjoyed blowing. He cautioned his men to wait for his signal, but they galloped to the attack when they saw him reach for the bugle.

The ten-wagon train carried corn west toward Fort Griffin. When the teamsters saw the Indians, they tried to turn their wagons into a circular corral, but the "screaming savages" reached them before they completed the circle.

Killing an enemy was important to an Indian, but to be first to touch him—counting coup—conferred even more honor. Big Tree made the first coup. Three or four teamsters were killed in the initial onslaught. Some saw an opening in the ring of attackers and broke through it. Only a few Indians followed the fleeing teamsters; they knew they would find plenty more in the circle of wagons. The battle did not last long. Seven teamsters were killed; five escaped. The Indians lost three.

Nothing credible indicates that Satanta or Satank took an active part in the combat. Yellow Wolf, last survivor of the raid, was interviewed by Lt. Col. W. S. Nye. The old Indian, who had ridden just ahead of Big Tree in the attack, had always insisted that Owl Prophet was the leader. Lone Wolf, not a chief at that time, made the second coup. He said that Satanta may have been blowing his bugle during the battle, but if so, no one paid attention. Satanta and Satank did not need any more coups.

By the time the Indians had returned to Fort Sill, the army knew of the wagon train battle. General Sherman was still at the fort, and he probably realized how lucky he was to still be alive. When the leading chiefs came to the commissary for their rations on May 27, Indian Agent Lawrie Tatum called them into his office and asked them if they knew anything about the raid on the wagon train. After a short silence, Satanta bragged, "I led that raid. You've been stealing our goods and giving them to the Texans; you've refused to give us arms so we can hunt buffalo, and you do not listen to our requests. I took a hundred of our warriors with Satank, Eagle Heart, Big Tree, Big Bow, and Fast

Bear . . ." Satank interrupted him, speaking roughly in Kiowa to not disclose any more names.

Tatum immediately took the chiefs to General Sherman, where discussion continued on their involvement in the raid. General Sherman's journal of his journey, as kept by General Randolph Marcy and quoted in *Indian Depredations in Texas*, contains a note supporting Satanta's later claim of no active involvement, despite his boast. The entry for May 27, after including Satanta's so-called admission, contains this note:

> *NOTE BY GENERAL SHERMAN*—The conversation
> with Satanta was through an interpreter. I understood
> him to say he took no part in the fight except to blow
> his trumpet. At that instant of time he had an ordinary
> trumpet slung on his person. W. T. S.

The army arrested Satanta, Satank, and Big Tree at the request of agent Tatum. Satanta argued in vain that he had lost three warriors with four more badly wounded, so the Kiowas and the whites were even. An army detail picked up the chiefs to deliver them to the civil authorities in Texas. Satank began singing his death song, saying he would not leave the place where his son's bones were buried. As the wagons rumbled away, the soldiers began mocking his song. Suddenly he jumped up and tried to grab a carbine with his handcuffed hands. He was shot several times and left on the road bleeding heavily from his mouth. He died within a few minutes.

Shortly after their delivery to the post guardhouse in Fort Richardson, Satanta and Big Tree were indicted for murder. The trial was set before Judge Charles Soward in Jacksboro, the county seat of Jack County. The attack had occurred in adjoining Young County, but that county government had been shut down for the Civil War and had not yet been reorganized. When the Jack County District Attorney, twenty-four-year-old S. W. T. Lanham, found out how little evidence he had, he sent five citizens to Fort Sill to get more. They talked to Tatum, and he told them about Satanta's admission that he and Big Tree had led the raid.

Tatum did not want to go to Texas to testify. "I put the confession in a letter to Colonel Grierson at the post," Tatum said. "Why can't you put it in evidence so I won't have to go?"

The letter, when found, did not mention Big Tree. When this was pointed out to Tatum, he said, "I'm sure Big Tree is guilty."

"Then why don't you copy the letter over and add his name," a Jacksboro citizen proposed.

Tatum did that, and the doctored letter became part of the evidence at the trial. Years later the original letter, found in General Sherman's papers in the Library of Congress, established that the evidence had been altered.

The court appointed Joseph A. Woolfolk to defend the Indians, with Thomas Ball assisting. When Woolfolk saw the list of fifty men summoned as potential jurors, he recognized one whose sister had been killed and another whose brother-in-law had been killed in Indian attacks. Judge Soward said he had noticed that, and "no, there will be no challenges to the jury panel."

When the trial began on July 5, Woolfolk protested that the court had no jurisdiction over an offense occurring in another county.

"Of course it has jurisdiction," district attorney Lanham argued. "Surely defense counsel is not suggesting that Jack County jurors cannot be fair and impartial."

Kiowa Chief Satanta. *Reproduced from the collections of the Library of Congress*

Judge Soward accepted that response and ruled for the district attorney.

Then Woolfolk surprised the court by asking that his clients be given separate trials. The judge invited the attorneys into his crowded office.

"Joe, what the hell are you doing?" asked Soward.

"A hundred or so men commit murder," Woolfolk replied. "You think you've got the leaders. Satanta is about fifty, and Big Tree is half his age. I don't know what else I'm doing, but I'm going to try and save the young one's life. He's entitled to a separate trial."

"You think I'm going to tell the army to double their guard and take one back? Haul them in one at a time?"

"I'm going to appeal this case."

"Like hell you are," said the judge.

"You wait and see."

"Indeed I will. We'll see if you have any records on which to base an appeal. Woolfolk, you must be crazy."

"Judge," Woolfolk pleaded, "Big Tree is a young man, and the evidence against him is not as strong as it is against Satanta. He never admitted anything. If he is tried first, he might have a chance with the jury. Then let another jury have their day against Satanta. He's already pretty old. Why can't you give Big Tree a fair chance?"

The Kiowas were the most expert tribe in sign language. That skill made them the best traders among the Plains Indians. Although Satanta could not speak English, he realized by now that Woolfolk was on his side. If he had understood English, he would have been baffled at the disparity between the procedure followed at his trial and ordinary common sense.

Once during the trial Satanta was reported to have said: "Many times we've sold captive children back to the whites. The whites must have known that Indians had killed the parents; yet they paid us money. Why are they now so mad that a few teamsters have gone to the spirit land?" He shook his head sadly. "How does one understand such people?"

Surprisingly, Judge Soward announced when they returned to the courtroom that the trials would be severed and Big Tree would be tried first.

"You handle this one," Woolfolk said to Ball. "I'll stick with Satanta."

The evidence was completed by early afternoon. After a long summation by the district attorney and a shorter one by Ball, the jury found Big Tree guilty and said he should be hanged.

Satanta's trial the next day took even less time. The judge shocked Woolfolk by saying he would use the same jury. This ignored the reason lawyers would give today for having separate trials—an independent adjudication by a different fact finder. The district attorney produced only one witness, who testified that he overheard Satanta admitting that he had led the raid. The jury was allowed to consider all the evidence they had heard the day before, and they returned the same verdict.

Judge Soward convened court the next morning for sentencing. He asked if the prisoners had anything to say. Ball shook his head for Big Tree. Woolfolk asked for an interpreter as his client did want to speak.

Satanta chose to speak in Comanche, the interpreter's best Indian language. "I have never been so near the Tehanos (Texans) before. I look around me and see your men, women, and children, and I have said in my heart that if I ever get back to my people I will not again make war upon you.

"I have tried to find friendship with the white man since I was so high." He held his hands at waist level. "My tribe has even taunted me and called me a woman because I associated with the whites.

"I did not kill the Tehanos. I came down to Pease River, where we began the raid, as a medicine man to doctor the wounds of the braves.

"I am an important chief among my people and have great influence among the warriors of my tribe; they know my voice and will hear my word.

"If you let me go back to my people, I will withdraw all warriors from Texas. I will take them all across the Red River and that shall be the line between us and the palefaces.

"I will wash out the spots of blood and make it a white land and there shall be peace, and the Tehanos may plow and drive their cattle to the banks of Red River. But if you kill me, it will be like a spark on the prairie. It will make a big fire. A terrible fire."

After a moment of silence he sat down.

Judge Soward sentenced each man "to hang by the neck until he is dead, dead, dead! And may God have mercy on his soul. Amen!"

As early as May 1877, the District Court of Jack County, where the trial was held, reported that all the papers in the case had been lost (they have never been found), so we are not as sure of what happened in the trial as we are of later developments. On August 2, 1871, Governor Edmund J. Davis commuted both sentences to life at hard labor, referring to Judge Soward's request dated July 10. The judge's request for commutation must have accompanied his report of the verdict.

Satanta's jury obviously thought he had led the raid in the same sense that Colonel Ben Grierson—then commanding Fort Sill—had earlier led his famous cavalry raid into the South in the Civil War. But Indian warriors, unlike cavalrymen, did not follow orders in battle. Each sought personal renown by counting coups. Their chiefs functioned more as recruiters and what modern whites would call tour leaders. After a warrior had counted enough coups, he could gather other young men to follow him on a raid. He would select the opponent and the time and place of attack, but he would say nothing about the mechanics of the attack. Having no need to count further coup, the chief could stand apart to help the wounded or pray to his personal gods to help his warriors as Satanta said he did. For these reasons small groups of disciplined soldiers or militia could defeat much larger groups of unorganized individuals seeking only personal glory. This variance in warfare started with the Puritans fighting New England Indians in King Phillip's War and continued for two and a half centuries to the end of the Indian Wars a few decades after the Warren Wagon Train Raid.

Whatever Satanta had said in his Kiowa, Comanche, Kiowa-Apache, Cheyenne, or Spanish languages got translated into a very different meaning in English. It is understandable that whites who spoke only English believed that leading a raid meant what they thought leadership meant—not just giving young warriors the opportunity to gain renown but to direct the manner in which it would be done.

On August 19, 1873, the Texas Penitentiary transferred both Satanta and Big Tree to the custody of the army, which took them to Fort Sill and put them in the guardhouse. A few weeks later Governor Davis came to the fort for a council, seeking peace between Texans and the Kiowas and Comanches.

A touching moment came when Satanta's aged father appeared and appealed to Davis to release his son.

"I am a poor old man," he said. "I want you to pity me and give up my son. The Indians love their children as much as the white people do theirs. You have your wife and children. Take pity on me; gladden my heart by the immediate release of my son. Never again will we raid upon Texas."

Davis listed the conditions to be met before he would release the two prisoners. Lone Wolf, the Kiowas' principal chief at that time, responded:

"This is a good day. I have heard the speech of the governor of Texas, and I and my young men have taken it all up. I looked through it for something bad. It is the very talk I would make to these people myself. My friends, you have come a long way to make a good road. You have already made our hearts good by bringing back these prisoners. Make them still better by releasing them today."

Other chiefs from the Kiowa-Apaches and the Comanches added their pleas for the release. On October 6, 1873, Governor Davis finally released the two prisoners to their people. They were paroled but not pardoned. The tribes were warned that any raiding by them would revoke the parole of Satanta and Big Tree, thus turning them into hostages to guarantee the behavior of the others. In fact the Comanche and Kiowa-Apache tribes each had to deliver five hostages to be held as security that those tribes would comply with the conditions imposed on the release of Satanta and Big Tree.

Despite the warnings about keeping the peace, the raids resumed before the end of the month. By the summer of 1874, raiding in western Oklahoma Territory and the Texas Panhandle had become widespread as the Indians tried to halt the destruction of the buffalo herds.

Satanta fought in the attack by Kiowas, Comanches, and Kiowa-Apaches on buffalo hunters at Adobe Walls on June 27, 1874. Cheyennes and Arapahoes also took the warpath in the growing conflict that widened into the Red River War. Satanta was in Woman's Heart's band late in August. He had resigned his chieftainship in early July in appreciation, he said, for his release. He and Big Tree surrendered with Woman's Heart's band on October 4. Satanta was immediately returned to Texas as a parole violator. Satanta's health declined after his return to prison. On October 18, 1878, he leaped headfirst out a second-story window in the prison hospital and landed on a brick wall below. The Indian Patrick Henry, the Kiowas' Winston Churchill, was dead.

Big Tree was held for a while after his surrender and then released, as the army determined that he had not violated his parole. After Satanta's suicide, Big Tree became the acknowledged leader of the Kiowa tribe. He lived fifty-five more years, thirty of them as a deacon in the Baptist Church. He died in 1929, aged eighty-four.

Misdirected Vengeance from "Those Californians"

"When I grow up," Sostenes L'Archévèque vowed, "I'll kill every white man I can." He had a Mexican-Indian mother, and he had seen his French father slain by an American at Sapello in eastern New Mexico. His intense hatred increased as he grew to maturity. At six feet, four inches, he moved like a panther, but his hooded eyes observed white men like a cobra.

L'Archévèque inherited his love of violence from his great grandfather's great grandfather, Jean L'Archévèque, who was thirteen in 1684 when he left France with one hundred explorers commanded by Robert de la Salle. They searched for the mouth of the Mississippi River, and three years later had still not found it. Then, on the Trinity River in Texas, the sixteen-year-old Jean diverted La Salle's attention while others in the party murdered their leader. The assassins argued, separating into two groups. Eventually the one headed by Hiens, an old German pirate, killed some of the other group. They wanted to kill Jean L'Archévèque, but he was away hunting at the time.

Only six of La Salle's one hundred men survived the journey to the New World, but they included Jean, who eventually reached New Mexico and served in the army at the Presidio of Santa Fe. He joined the ill-fated Pedro de Villasur expedition of 1720, which reached further into the interior of North America than any other Spanish expedition. Pawnees killed most of the expedition, including Jean, when it reached the Platte River.

In the 1870s L'Archévèque's operating grounds were around Old Tascosa in the Canadian River valley of the Texas Panhandle. He shared this territory with a more publicized outlaw from New Mexico, Billy the Kid. Most of the law-abiding folks thought Billy the Kid an amateur compared to L'Archévèque. This judgment was not based on the number of notches in their guns—each would have from twenty to twenty-five by the time he was killed—but on their motivation.

Brooklyn-born Billy the Kid wanted to avenge the murder of the only man who had ever treated him decently. He became a hero to many Westerners. L'Archévèque was a hero to no one; he just wanted to kill all the Anglos he could. The way that he killed three sheepmen in 1876 should hold the record for perfidy and villainy in the Old West. Out of disgust, his own brother-in-law finally killed him to protect the community.

John Casner and his three sons had hit it rich in the California gold rush. John and his son Lew moved on to Silver City, New Mexico, to prospect. The other brothers took their share, had a thousand $20 gold pieces minted at Carson City, and invested the rest in 1,600 sheep. Their search for good sheep country brought them and their flock to the Texas Panhandle.

While Miguel García herded three thousand sheep near the place where Wildorado Creek flowed out of high mountains toward the Canadian River that summer of 1876, he saw the Casner flock in the distance. The Casner brothers, with a Navajo Indian boy employed as herder, were slowly moving their sheep toward the free grass of the Palo Duro country.

Miguel welcomed the Casner brothers and told them that they were only about thirty miles from their destination. He admired their sheep and equipment and thought they might be rich. Soon other men met the new sheepmen, slowly herding their way through. They referred to them as "Those Californians."

Colás Martínez, boss of the Canadian River country, had been an Indian fighter and a store operator; now he had the largest flock of sheep in the area. He, too, welcomed the Casner brothers and told them they would find good grazing land a week or so on ahead. That very spring Charles Goodnight, Texas's leading cattleman, had ridden into the Palo Duro country seeking cattle range, and Colás had helped him look the country over and pick out the place for his ranch headquarters.

The one bane of Colás's life was the outlaw L'Archévèque, who had married his sister. The señoritas thought L'Archévèque, a tall, lithe blond, was handsome, but what an accumulation of pure hate to have marry into one's family! Goodnight would become the most powerful force for law and order in the Panhandle, and he discussed L'Archévèque and his reputation with Colás.

"Don't worry, Colonel," Colás said. "I will kill him myself if he makes more trouble."

L'Archévèque persuaded a Mexican boy, Ysabel Gurules, to go with him on a hunting trip. Instead, he led the way directly to the Casner brothers' sheep camp. Only one of the brothers was present. L'Archévèque talked to the man long enough to learn that the other brother and their Indian herder were away with the sheep. Then L'Archévèque shot him dead.

Ysabel cried and begged L'Archévèque to let him ride away. L'Archévèque slapped the boy until he agreed to hide while L'Archévèque waited for the second brother to return to camp.

When the second brother arrived, L'Archévèque shot him as he rode up to his tent. Then L'Archévèque ordered Ysabel to find the Indian herder and kill him. Shaking with fear, the boy started crying again, and L'Archévèque beat him. The boy ran, jumped on the faster of their two horses, and galloped away. He was out of gun range when L'Archévèque realized that he was going home instead of following instructions; but the old nag left by the boy was too slow to catch the faster horse.

L'Archévèque decided that it was best that Ysabel had gone. He had only found a few gold pieces on the bodies of the two brothers he had killed. He would have to force the Indian to talk before he killed him. He did not want Ysabel there when he collected the rest of the gold.

The Indian herder, with the sheepdogs, was moving the flock toward the camp when L'Archévèque rode out to meet him. The herder, though frightened, refused to reveal any information. L'Archévèque shoved his pistol into the boy's stomach.

"You tell me where the gold is hidden or you'll die right here and right quick," he snarled.

One of the dogs attacked, knocking L'Archévèque off balance. He recovered, shot the dog, and again demanded that the Indian boy tell him where the gold was.

The boy told him where part of the treasure was hidden, but he did not know about the rest. "They put it in lots of places," the boy stammered. "I only know of the one."

Convinced that the boy told the truth and that no more information could be had, L'Archévèque clubbed him to death with his pistol. While he did this, the other dog attacked. He shot that one to death. The first dog was still unconscious.

L'Archévèque left the bloody scene and returned to the camp, where he found one leather bag full of gold pieces near a spring. Then L'Archévèque roped one of the two dead bodies in the camp and dragged it to the edge of a rock cliff, where he kicked it off, watching it roll and bounce to some bushes below. He took one of the Casner pistols and rode back to Tascosa. When L'Archévèque learned that Ysabel had told others of L'Archévèque's plan to kill the Californians, he decided to hide out a while.

Colás Martínez intended to keep his promise to Colonel Goodnight. He called a meeting of the men in the community, and they agreed that L'Archévèque should be killed. They set a trap by sending word to L'Archévèque that he could find food if he came to the house of Felix Gurules, Ysabel's uncle.

When L'Archévèque crept into the Gurules adobe that evening, Felix Gurules and Miguel García, hiding inside the door, grabbed his arms and stabbed him in the back. Then Colás stepped into the room, cursed L'Archévèque, and shot him twice at point-blank range. Even then the enraged L'Archévèque continued to struggle.

"Pull that knife out of my back, and I'll kill all you bastards," he screamed.

Colás pounded the wounded man's head with his pistol until he slumped into unconsciousness. A few seconds later L'Archévèque revived. He lunged and struggled, trying to get to his feet. He screamed and cursed, calling down all the evil spirits he could remember to help him attack his enemies.

One of the men tried to choke L'Archévèque; another pounded his head again with the pistol. Barely dazed, L'Archévèque still fought and cursed. Then the third man saw a gold chain around L'Archévèque's neck with something like a cross on it. He ripped it off, and L'Archévèque dropped into unconsciousness. He died the next morning. Besides the three men who attacked L'Archévèque, Sacramento Baca, Francisco Nolan, Agapito Gurules, and one Florentine had watched the gruesome battle.

L'Archévèque was buried on the south bank of the Canadian, in an unmarked grave. Although the hate-filled killer finally lay dead, the incident had not ended. About a week later, two of Goodnight's cowboys rode into the abandoned sheep camp, where they saw the body of one of the Casner brothers. They also saw the dog that, with one eye shot out, was still faithfully protecting the sheep. The cowboys moved the sheep down the canyon and turned them over to Dave McCormick, who hated sheep and sheepherders. But McCormick loved dogs, and he soon appreciated his new and intelligent friend and helped him herd the sheep.

When Goodnight returned to Pueblo, Colorado, where he was living at the time, he described the property of the Casner brothers, which had been found, and requested that the news of the killings be published in western newspapers. Two Texans prospecting in Silver City, New Mexico, with John and Lew Casner read the account, and the four men went to the Panhandle to investigate. The Casners had no trouble proving their right to the sheep, and they paid Goodnight for their keep, apparently planning to take them away.

Then rumors arose that the surviving Casners, their Texan miners, and other Texan friends planned to drive all Mexicans out of the Canadian River valley. Goodnight warned them that his well-armed cowboys would prevent such wholesale reprisals. The Casners gave up the grandiose plan but decided to kill everyone directly involved in the murder of the brothers.

Deciding that the best way to find their targets was to look for the brothers' gold coins, the Casners challenged all comers to a horse race in Tascosa and bet $500 on the outcome. Colás Martínez won the race, but the Casners identified some of the money put up by his backers as coins minted by the brothers. They hired Colás and Felix Gurules to guide them into a canyon for a look at the country.

Twelve miles into the canyon, the Casners and their Texan friends suddenly drew their guns and fired, hitting Colás in the hand. Colás shot one of the Texans in the stomach, and Gurules raced away for his life. Then the wounded Texan shot again

Cliffs above Canadian River at Tascosa, Texas, near where L'Archévèque killed the Casner brothers. *Author's photo collection*

before he died, this time killing Colás. The Casners watched their wounded friend die and then resolved to go to the place where the brothers had been killed, hoping to intercept the fleeing Felix Gurules there. They did not know that they had already killed the man who had killed the murderer of the brothers.

Felix Gurules reached the camp where his nephew Ysabel was tending other sheep. Before the Guruleses could get away, the pursuing Casners rode up and shot Felix down in a hail of bullets. Ysabel again begged for his life, and eventually one of the Casners persuaded the others that they should not kill a boy.

But the Casners and their vengeance-minded gang still had men to hunt down and kill. The next day they hanged Agapito Nolan and Florentine from a chinaberry tree, unaware that their victims had been present and approving when the murderer of the brothers had been killed.

Another Mexican, who apparently planned to steal the sheep after the brothers were killed, turned himself in at Fort Elliott for protection. The determined Casners hired five off-duty black cavalrymen to capture the man from his military guard. The next morning the man was found hanging from a cottonwood tree.

Then the Casner gang found Colás's sister (L'Archévèque's widow) and took the money her brother had won in the horse race. That money probably included coins that Colás had taken from L'Archévèque when he killed him, money that the Casners thought proved that Colás was involved in stealing their sheep.

For years afterward when Mexican sheepmen were asked why they had moved out of the Canadian River valley of the Texas Panhandle to return to northeastern New Mexico, fear would cloud their faces and they would shake their heads and mutter, "Those Californians."

He Was a Man before He Was Done Being a Boy

Believe-It-or-Not Robert Ripley may have exaggerated in claiming that Bill Longley had been hanged three times. Longley, of course, should have known, and the second time he had a noose around his neck he did say, "Hanging is my favorite way of dying. I'd rather die that way than any other way except a natural death."

When Sheriff J. M. Brown sprung the trap on October 11, 1878, in Giddings, Texas, the noose slipped, and Longley dropped to his knees. He was hoisted up and dropped again, so one can see why Ripley made the claim about three hangings. Nine years before, vigilantes had also tried to hang the man. Longley, finally doing his last dance in the air, was just six days past his twenty-seventh birthday.

Born October 5, 1851, William Preston Longley grew up on the family farm in what would become Lee County, a few miles from Giddings, and learned early to use guns. He would become one of the fastest draws in Texas.

The first of the nation's modern gunslingers, Longley differed from most Texas outlaws in that he was not a robber or cattle rustler, and was never part of a gang. He generally played a lone hand. His distinguishing mark seemed to be his pure enjoyment in the act of killing.

The reconstruction effort after the Civil War included the creation of a state police in Texas, made up mostly of freed slaves.

Most Southerners, including Texans from the eastern part of the state, nursed bitterness about the war and hated reconstruction. In December 1866, shortly after his fifteenth birthday, Bill and his father were in town when a black policeman, waving his gun, insulted Bill's father. Perhaps the black man didn't know that Bill's father was a staunch Unionist—a clear minority in east Texas. The elder Longley's sterling record at the Battle of San Jacinto warded off criticism from his white neighbors.

Bill, carrying his usual pistol, stepped forward. "You put that gun down," he said.

The policeman pointed his gun at Bill, and Bill shot him dead. Bill joined other young men and began to terrorize the newly freed slaves. He was already six feet tall, with curly black hair and a high-cheekboned, angular face, and his small, fierce black eyes smoldered with hate. During 1867 Bill killed at least three and perhaps five black men.

In 1869, near Yorktown, Texas, Bill was mistaken for his brother-in-law and friend, Charley Taylor, one of the leaders in the Sutton-Taylor feud. Black army troops had been ordered into the area to put down violence. Some soldiers, thinking Bill was a Taylor, approached to make an arrest. Bill thought they wanted him for his most recent killing, and he fled. Bill Longley rode like a Comanche, and after six miles he had out-distanced all but the sergeant in charge, who was mounted as well as he. Longley had only one bullet left when the sergeant pulled abreast. He jammed his pistol into the sergeant's side and pulled the trigger. The soldier fell dead from his saddle, and Longley escaped.

Now Longley preyed on freed slaves and Union soldiers in black regiments who were traveling alone. One evening, vigilantes caught him and a horse thief named Tom Johnson, who had joined Longley at his campfire. Believing that birds of a feather flocked together, the vigilantes strung both men up. Longley, just sixteen with five notches already in his pistol, found himself face-to-face with death. But as the vigilantes rode away, they fired their pistols toward their victims in the customary celebration. One of the bullets struck Longley's rope before he died, his heavy body broke the rope, and he recovered from his first hanging. Johnson wasn't so lucky.

By this time Longley was Texas's most wanted outlaw. His aged parents begged him to leave the state. Later that year he joined a trail herd to Abilene, bossed by a man named Rector.

After they reached Indian Territory and Rector got his crew to pitch in and buy a keg of liquor, Rector got into a shooting scrape with one of the men, wounding him in the shoulder. The next day Longley remarked that Rector had better not treat him that way or he would regret it. Rector, hearing about the remark, rode up to face Longley.

"I understand, damn you," Rector said, "that you said I had better not run on to you. Is that so?"

"As sure as hell," Longley answered calmly, "I damn sure did say them very words."

Rector went for his pistol, but Longley beat him to the draw. Longley had six bullets in Rector's body before the trail boss started to slide out of the saddle, dead.

The trail crew advised Longley to give himself up at Fort Sill, as the authorities would surely let him go on their evidence that Rector had started the fight. But Longley was afraid the authorities would discover that he was wanted in Texas, so he rode on, joined by a cowboy named Davis who volunteered to ride with him.

ADVENTURES
—OF—
BILL LONGLEY

Captured by Sheriff Milton Mast and Deputy Bill
Burrows, near Keatchie, Louisiana, in
1877, and was executed at
Giddings, Texas,
1878.

BILL BURROWS - LONGLEY - SHERIFF MAST

By Henry C. Fuller
Nacogdoches, Texas

Photograph of the captured Bill Longley. *Reproduced from the collections of the Library of Congress*

One night, five Osage Indians tried to steal horses from Longley and Davis. The men killed one Indian; the other four ran. After visiting Abilene, Kansas, for a few days, Longley went on to Fort Leavenworth, where he got into an argument in a saloon with a soldier who had asked him if he was from Texas.

"Yes, I'm from Texas," Longley answered.

"Well, now," the trooper snarled, "if I was from Texas I'd be damned ashamed of it and keep it to myself. I know from firsthand experience that there's not an honest man in Texas nor a virtuous woman either."

Later Longley would say, "Before the words were cold on his lips, I sent a bullet through his heart, and when several of his companions made a move as to interfere, I covered them and informed them that if they did not want to get a quick pass to hell, to keep quiet."

Bill took the train to St. Joseph, where two armed officers grabbed him and said he was under arrest for killing the soldier in the saloon. Three weeks later he bribed the sergeant in charge of the guardhouse with $50 and a violin he had carved out of soft wood, and Bill escaped.

Bill Longley spent the next two years as a miner, mountain man, gambler, and teamster in Wyoming. He killed a man at Camp Brown (later called Fort Washakie) and got a thirty-year sentence in federal prison. Again he escaped and rode south to Colorado, where he lived a year with the Ute Indians.

Lonesome now for Texas, Bill headed for the Kansas trail towns, hoping to find a way to ride back to his home. At Parkerville, Kansas, a small town near the Santa Fe Trail, he shot a man to death in a gambling hall. The victim's father offered a $1,500 reward. Bill and two others, also on the dodge, cooked up a scheme in which the two companions turned Bill in for the reward and then sprung him from the jail. They divided the money evenly and rode their separate ways, Bill going back to Texas.

By this time his parents had moved a short way north to Belton, and Bill spent some time with them. But he learned that a Lee County posse was coming to arrest him for a $1,000 reward, and he again hit the Owl Hoot Trail. Soon a black man who'd gotten drunk and insulted a white woman lay dead with two of Bill's bullets in his head. Bill continued riding west.

Five men caught up with him in the Santa Anna Mountains of Coleman County. After a short battle in which Bill killed one, the other four withdrew. It was now late in 1874, and Bill returned to Central Texas, took the name Jim Patterson, and went to work in a cotton gin. But he got into an argument with a George Thomas and shot him through the heart. He stopped in Bell County long enough to hug his old mother and shake the trembling hand of his father. Deeply conscious of the worry he had caused them, he rode southwest to a lonely ranch in the Frio Canyon of Bandera County. He was just beginning to think about settling down in that beautiful canyon when he learned that a recent friend, Lon Sawyer, was scheming with the sheriff back in Lee County to turn Bill in for half the offered reward.

At first Bill considered just shooting Sawyer, but he learned that a reward had been offered for Sawyer, and Bill decided to turn the tables on him. Bill got himself deputized by the Uvalde County sheriff to bring Sawyer in. Bill, in turn, deputized a youth named Hayes to help him capture Sawyer.

An unsuspecting Sawyer, still waiting to hear from the Lee County sheriff, cantered leisurely down a trail with Longley, Hayes, and a wagon to cut up a steer that Longley and Sawyer had recently stolen and killed. Suddenly Longley leveled his pistol at Sawyer and shouted: "Throw up your hands. You're my prisoner."

"I'll see you in hell, first," Sawyer shouted back, drawing his own weapon and spurring his horse forward.

Longley's first bullet hit Sawyer's shoulder, and Sawyer's bullet missed, as the two men began one of the West's wildest shooting rides. They rode through a cedar brake and burst into a glade about two hundred yards long. When they reached the end of the glade, both pistols were empty, Longley was still untouched, and Sawyer had three more bullets in his back. One of the two bullets fired by Longley, which missed Sawyer, disabled Sawyer's horse. Sawyer drew his shotgun, leaped to the ground, and killed Longley's horse. Then Sawyer disappeared into another dense cedar brake.

Bill had a second pistol, but the caps had gotten wet and wouldn't fire. He ran back toward the approaching wagon, where he knew the teamster had a gun. On the way he met Hayes and told him he could follow Sawyer's trail from the blood spurting out of his four back wounds.

Learning that the teamster only had a carbine with three cartridges, Longley unharnessed one of the wagon horses, jumped on its back, and plunged through the cedar brake to cut Sawyer off. In the meantime a pack of hounds, attracted by the noise, were assailing Longley.

Suddenly Sawyer, lying on the ground, fired his shotgun and barely missed Longley. Longley jumped to the ground and fired at Sawyer. He hit the man's shotgun stock and spun around to shoot two of the closest hounds. Then Longley took his time to reload his good pistol.

After Longley fired eight more times and Sawyer six, Sawyer called out that he wanted to talk things over.

"Not unless you throw your pistol out," Longley replied.

Sawyer did that, and Longley walked over to where he lay, weak from loss of blood. But Sawyer had another pistol that Longley didn't know about. He fired it but missed. Longley's shot, fired so simultaneously to his opponent's that they sounded like one roar, hit Sawyer above the eyes, killing him instantly.

Sawyer's last shot had hit Hayes in the leg as he arrived at the battle scene. Sawyer had fired fourteen shots, and only killed Bill's horse. Longley had fired eighteen times, hitting Sawyer thirteen times, besides killing his horse and five dogs. Longley said Sawyer was the bravest man he had ever fought. Longley's short career in Texas law enforcement was over.

Later in 1875, Longley learned that a boyhood friend, Wilson Anderson, had killed Bill's nephew, Cale Longley, in Bastrop County, near where Bill grew up. Joined by his brother James, Longley rode directly to Anderson's farm, found his old friend plowing in the field, and gunned him down with a shotgun. This was the murder that would result in Longley's eventual execution.

After the Anderson killing the Longley brothers fled to Indian Territory and then returned to Texas. James turned himself in and was acquitted of any part in Anderson's murder. Bill Longley stayed on the loose. He was captured in Edwards County by Sheriff Bill Henry. Henry took his prisoner to Austin to collect the reward, but when the governor refused to pay it, Sheriff Henry turned Longley loose.

On February 12, 1876, Bill Longley was riding through Delta County in northeast Texas when he met Louvenia Jack at a small farm near Ben Franklin. Falling in love for the only time in his life, he introduced himself as William Black of Missouri, saying he had lived in Texas about three years.

"We sat up late that night," Bill would write later from jail. "I never felt such feelings on earth as now seemed to take possession of me. I lay and thought of all my past life, and never before did I realize my true condition. I thought I would give all the wealth in the world, if I had it to give, if I was only a plain, civil, and pious man. I thought I would get up an excuse so I could stop and rest for a day or two, and perhaps in that time I could make up my mind what I should do."

Later Bill got out of bed in the Jack home, retrieved a nail from the fireplace, and hammered it into his horse's hoof. After breakfast he "discovered" that his lame horse could not travel, so Mr. Jack invited him to stay over a day or two. Then sixteen-year-old Louvenia suggested that Bill "Black" talk to a preacher, Roland Lay, who lived a mile away and needed someone to farm his place on shares. Jack thought the idea great, and the arrangements with Preacher Lay soon were worked out.

Bill had always enjoyed working the soil, and now he was only a mile from the love of his life. But he soon learned that the preacher's cousin also had designs on Louvenia. In fact, they had been engaged to be married when Mr. and Mrs. Jack opposed the match.

Bill had taken a great liking to the preacher, and he was shocked to learn that the preacher was the main one encouraging his cousin to resume his attempt to win Louvenia. Three months after he had been living in the preacher's cabin and farming the land, Bill found a note tied to the plow handles, warning him to leave the county. To a cold-blooded killer like Bill Longley, such a note was an invitation to violence. Yet Bill, for the first time in his life, did something noble: He rode away and found work on another farm, ten miles away in Lamar County.

Some days later, while Bill was visiting the Jacks, one of the Lay family killed a Jack dog, and Bill horsewhipped him. Preacher Lay responded by getting a warrant from Lamar County, saying Bill had threatened his life. Bill escaped from the Lamar County jail by burning it down. He reached the Jack cabin just before dawn, grabbed their shotgun from their mantel, rode to Lay's and found the preacher in the cow pen, milking. A double-barreled, heavy load of turkey shot left the community without a preacher. But this time Bill had killed an old, unarmed man, who had an infant daughter asleep in her crib inside the house. Bill knew he had to ride far away.

Bill crossed into Indian Territory, riding past the house where Jim Reed, outlaw husband of Belle Starr, had been killed two years before. He tried to stay away from people; sometimes he didn't see another person for a week at a time. Once, he traded his horse and shotgun to an Indian for the Indian's horse. The Indian changed his mind, caught up with Bill, and attacked him with a knife. Bill shot him in the forehead and again in the chest before the body hit the ground. Then Bill found two improved Colt's cartridge pistols under the Indian's blanket and took them, since they were no use to a dead Indian.

Bill kept thinking of Louvenia back in Ben Franklin, and sometimes cried himself to sleep. He rode through northeast and east Texas, always keeping to himself, and finally reached De Soto Parish, Louisiana. There he made another sharecropping deal, this time as Will Jackson. He became friends with another farmer, June Courtney, who had just been elected town constable. Courtney often asked his new friend to help make arrests. Bill was so efficient as a helper that Courtney began studying wanted posters from Texas. Then Courtney tipped off the Nacogdoches County, Texas, sheriff that he thought he had Bill Longley in his town.

Using a carefully planned approach, the Texas sheriff, his deputy, and the Louisiana constable were able to take Longley into custody on May 11, 1877, without getting hurt.

Longley was tried in Giddings in September for the Anderson killing. On Monday, September 3, 1877, he was arraigned on a grand jury indictment. He pled not guilty and asked for a continuance. The court denied his motion and trial began the next morning at 8:30. Later that day jury foreman J. S. Wade signed a verdict of guilty. The court still had time to take up other matters that day. Longley was removed to Galveston to await the decision on his automatic appeal. While there he complained to the governor that it was unfair to execute him as he had only killed thirty-two men, and John Wesley Hardin received a life sentence for killing many more.

Bill wrote a lot and told a lot to reporters while he was in jail waiting for execution. He had only regretted one of his thirty-two killings. That victim was a cowboy on the trail to Kansas who seemed to be watching Bill too closely.

"I wasn't going to sleep with that fellow watching," Bill said. "So I shot him and then went to sleep. The next day I learned that he was on the dodge, just like me."

Longley came back in court on September 5, 1878, for formal pronouncement of judgment, his execution having been affirmed. The judge ordered "that you be by the sheriff of Lee County hung by the neck until you are dead, dead, dead."

Some detested Bill Longley because he killed for the love of killing. Others saw him as a heroic figure resisting a reconstruction that had been inflicted by an insensitive victor in war. Another judgment is contained in an oft-quoted statement about Longley: "He was a man before he was done being a boy."

Longley himself put it this way: "I have always known that I was doing wrong, but I got started when I was a fool boy, led off by older heads, and taught to believe that it was right to kill sassy Negroes, and then to resist military law."

When the noose was dropped over Bill's head in October 1878, just a few miles from where he had started as a fifteen-year-old killer, it was the second time he had felt one on his neck. This time, it still took two attempts to succeed.

A Woman Who Saw
Much of Life

Myra Belle Shirley, born in the southwest Missouri town of Carthage on February 5, 1848, inherited her love of violence. Her mother was a Hatfield, one of Kentucky's famous feuding families.

As a young girl Myra was small, pretty, and full of life, but she also displayed a fiery temper. Her parents operated a tavern that became a meeting place for Confederate soldiers, guerrillas, and bushwhackers during the Civil War. It provided a fine background for the development of one of the West's leading woman outlaws.

Myra was also smart. She entered the Carthage Female Academy when it was organized in 1855. One of the first to master the curriculum of reading, spelling, grammar, arithmetic, deportment, Greek, Latin, Hebrew, and music, Myra also learned to play the piano. A fellow student remembered her as intelligent but "of a fierce nature who would fight anyone, boy or girl, whom she quarreled with; otherwise she seemed a nice girl."

Myra loved horses and the outdoors. She became a fine rider and loved to roam the hills with her brother, John Allison (Bud), six years older. Bud Shirley, wild and daring and also an excellent rider, taught his eager sister how to handle a rifle and pistol.

Bud fought with local guerrillas, attacking antislavery neighbors and Union soldiers. He rode with a group of about forty men. Myra spied on Union troops to assist her brother's guerrilla band.

Belle Starr and Deputy US Marshal Tyner Hughes, May 23, 1886.
Research Division of the Oklahoma Historical Society, Barde Collection

William Quantrill rode into the area with his Border Ruffians, and one of his men met Myra in November 1862. Both fourteen-year-old Myra and sixteen-year-old Jim Reed instantly discovered a soul mate in the other. Reed, handy with fists and guns, had been riding with Quantrill for a year.

In February 1863, when she was fifteen, Myra learned that some neighbors were sheltering Union troops, and she got this information to her brother's guerrilla band. The band attacked the troops and drove them out, killing two or three.

The Confederate defeats at Vicksburg and Gettysburg later in 1863 convinced most that the Confederacy was doomed, but the guerrillas in southwest Missouri kept fighting. By early 1864 Bud Shirley was one of the men most wanted by

Union troops in Missouri. Near the end of June he was killed by men of the Third Wisconsin Cavalry, riding out of Fort Scott, Kansas.

Myra went with her father to claim her brother's body. As her father laid the body in their wagon, a squad of Union soldiers glowered with contempt. Someone laid Bud's cap and ball revolver on the seat next to Myra. The grief-stricken girl picked up her brother's pistol and began handling it.

"Put that gun down, Myra," her father ordered.

Myra glared at the soldiers and snatched the pistol out of its holster. "You damned blue-bellies will pay for this," she screamed.

As the onlookers scattered in panic, her father ran to the front of the wagon. But before he could reach Myra she had leveled the pistol at the soldiers and was thumbing the hammer as fast as she could.

The weapon only clicked; someone had removed the firing caps. As the wagon moved away, the soldiers laughed and Myra sobbed helplessly.

Impassioned feelings leading to neighbor on neighbor violence had often resulted in warnings to the Shirleys to leave the state, but they had held on stubbornly. On September 22, 1864, most of Carthage was burned and abandoned, including the tavern and home of the Shirleys. But the Shirleys had already left. Disheartened by the loss of his son, John Shirley loaded his family into two wagons and they moved to Scyene, Texas, a small village ten miles southeast of Dallas, where a cousin of the family and other Missourians had already settled. Sixteen-year-old Myra drove one of the wagons. Her fury at Yankees still burned like a fever.

The Shirleys started farming about a mile east of Scyene. They got off to a bad start. They lived in a dugout at first, then built a four-room house. Water had to be hauled in barrels from distant Trinity Creek. Neighbors complained that they took too much water and didn't leave enough for others. Remembering the violence between neighbors in Missouri, the Shirleys kept to themselves. The rough and hearty backslapping Texans thought them unsociable.

Myra attended the one-room community school but very irregularly. She had already mastered the courses at the female academy in Missouri, and she looked down on the other pupils. With her scathing tongue and fiery temper, the others thought her wild. She and fifteen-year-old brother Edwin helped care for the two younger boys. The family changed the name of seven-year-old Cravens to John Allison in memory of Bud. Myra's only entertainment was riding horseback along Mesquite Creek and collecting news from Missouri.

Frank and Jesse James, the Younger Brothers, and others from Quantrill's Raiders were now riding as a band of robbers, and Myra followed their news closely. Perhaps she would hear something of Jim Reed. The robbers could not use the gold they stole from railroads and banks because it was not functional in transactions by common people—it just became incriminating evidence. So six of them—including Jesse James and Cole Younger and at least three more Younger brothers—rode three hundred miles to San Antonio to sell their gold to a Mexican broker at a deep discount. On their return ride north in July 1866, they stopped at the Shirleys' for a short visit.

Some speculate that Cole Younger seduced Myra on this trip, but other than the fact that Myra's first child was said by some to be named Pearl Younger, there is no evidence to support the story. Myra Belle did say in an interview in later years that the first man she fell in love with and the first man she married was "a dashing guerrilla."

Belle's dashing guerrilla was Jim Reed. His father died in 1865, and his widowed mother moved with her children, including Jim, to Collin County, Texas, settling near McKinney, where a couple of relatives were living.

The Reeds and the Shirleys renewed old friendships, and love flamed anew in Belle and Jim. They married in Collin County on November 1, 1866. Jim moved in with his in-laws, helping with their farming. He considered buying land of his own, but when that fell through in 1867, he and Belle joined his mother and brothers and they all returned to Missouri to farm there.

Belle had a daughter, Rosie Lee, in September 1868. She idolized the child and called her "my little pearl." From this description by a loving mother has come—from writers more filled with imagination than facts—the story (and a book) that Belle's first child was Pearl Younger, illegitimate daughter of noted outlaw Cole Younger. Belle's parents and her brothers always called the child Rosie Lee.

Soon after the birth of his daughter, Jim Reed killed a man in Arkansas who had just killed Jim's younger brother. Jim fled to Indian Territory because the only lawmen there were United States marshals, and there weren't many of those.

In 1870, not feeling safe even in the Territory, Jim took his family and fled to Los Angeles, California. Jim rode horseback the whole distance, and Belle and Rosie Lee rode a stagecoach.

Belle often described her time in California as the happiest period of their lives. Their son Edward was born there in 1871.

In early 1872 Los Angeles police learned that Jim Reed was wanted in Arkansas. Again he fled, this time at night and again on horseback. Belle and the children traveled around Cape Horn on a sailing ship and took refuge with her parents, who had moved from the farm into Scyene. Jim reached them soon afterward, having ridden through the southwest United States and parts of Mexico.

The two families were crowded in a three-room house, but John Shirley had apparently prospered. He acquired a place in the country for his daughter and her family. Jim and Belle began managing a string of racehorses, and they did a lot of horse trading. Belle took care of the business end of their venture because Jim, with a price on his head, had to keep under cover.

Jim was often mixed up in deals involving stolen cattle and horses, but the community—then in the carpetbagger stage of Texas history—overlooked his faults. They treated him as an ex-soldier, persecuted by Yankees and carpetbaggers.

Once, Jim was thrown into jail in a little town, and Belle refused to leave him. The next day she visited the jail, dressed in a black dress and a heavy black veil. Later the jailer discovered that Jim had walked out, wearing Belle's costume. The "inmate" remaining in the jail was Belle!

"I have committed no crime," Belle told the jailer. "The Bible says that a woman should cleave to her husband, doesn't it? Well, I only did my duty."

Belle was kept in the cell for a few days and then released without charges.

About 1873 a Dallas County sheriff named Nichols put Jim in jail, and Belle threatened to kill the sheriff. The next day Nichols was shot dead in a Dallas street, and Belle was credited with the killing. Many newspapers reported the crime, and the *Kansas City Star* carried a drawing of Belle galloping furiously away from the murder surrounded by a hail of bullets. However, there is no record that Belle was ever charged with the killing. Jim was released soon after Nichols was slain.

Also in 1873, Jim Reed and Belle, dressed as a man, and two other men, all masked, robbed a rich Creek Indian, said to have stolen a large sum from tribal funds. The robbery occurred in the Indian's home in nearby Indian Territory. The four robbers tortured the Indian and his wife by putting ropes around their necks and hoisting them off the floor to make them talk. After the man had been "hanged" seven times and his wife three, they disclosed where $30,000 in gold was hidden. Soon after the robbery Belle came out with a new string of racehorses and her horses were accepted into all the big race meets throughout Texas.

Belle often disguised herself as a man. Shortly after the robbery of the Creek Indians, she was in the Riggs Hotel in Bonham, Texas, wearing a young man's clothing while the robbery was being discussed. When the discussion mentioned Belle and Jim, a Dallas lawyer spoke up. He said he knew Belle intimately and she was a "no good" woman. The hotel was crowded, and the lawyer had to share his bed that night with a "young man."

The next morning Belle told her bedmate, "Partner, I'm not a man. You tell your wife that you slept last night with Belle Reed!" One writer added the touch that she struck him with a riding whip as she stormed away contemptuously.

Another popular story about Belle related that during one of Jim's absences she set herself up in an unnamed Texas town as a rich Southern widow. She attended church regularly, patronized the town's leading dressmaker, milliner, and beauty parlor, and was soon accepted by the most respectable people, including a prominent banker. One night the late-working banker let Belle into his office. She drew a pistol, relieved the bank of $30,000 in greenbacks, and disappeared. Before leaving, she bound and gagged her victim. He had difficulty with explanations to his wife the next morning.

We have no proof of this story, but it sounds just like something Belle would enjoy doing.

We do have details of Belle's involvement in one of Texas's most notorious stage robberies. Sometime in February 1874, she and J. M. Dickson and his wife rented a house in San Antonio to study stage schedules and plan the robbery. On Thursday, April 1, the three moved to San Marcos and camped on the bank of the beautiful San Marcos River, probably at the site of present Aquarena Springs. The next day Jim Reed, the leader, joined them with Cal Carter and John Nelson.

Reed, Carter, and Nelson left the camp on Sunday, purchased some rather poor riding horses, and waited just north of the Blanco River, near present-day Kyle, Texas. On Tuesday evening, April 7, they held up the San Antonio to Austin stage about two miles north of the Blanco station. The nine passengers included the president and teller of the San Antonio National Bank, the president's brother, two other San Antonio businessmen, two discharged soldiers, a lady from St. Paul, Minnesota, a man from Fort Concho, and a young German who had just boarded the stage in San Marcos.

The robbers moved their saddles to the better-quality stage horses and rode east toward Lockhart. Then they doubled back northwest toward Fort Concho, before the trail was lost.

Besides $1,000 from the bank president (who hid his watch in the grass), they got smaller amounts of cash and jewelry from all the others. The total of cash was $2,500, and mail sacks were also taken.

The next day the Texas legislature met and authorized a reward of $3,000. Others added to the reward until it reached $7,000.

When the United States marshal questioned the three campers left behind, Belle gave her name as Rosa McComus. This was the name of an acquaintance of Belle's whom she did not like because of her stuck-up attitude. Belle often used that alias with impish delight.

Belle and the Dicksons were examined by the United States magistrate but released without being charged.

Later in August 1874, Jim Reed was shot to death by John Morris in a Collin County farmhouse. Morris was an acquaintance of Jim, and the two men were traveling together when they stopped at the farmhouse for a meal.

Jim usually carried a repeating carbine as a saddle gun. This time he entered the house unarmed, as it appeared that Morris had persuaded him that the farmer was squeamish about having weapons in his house. So Jim left his pistol belt on his saddle, and he leaned his carbine against the house, just outside the door. Morris also entered unarmed, but then slipped out, got his own pistol, and returned to shoot Jim in the back for the dead-or-alive reward then being offered for the robbery of the stage. Different versions of the killing differ in details, but there is no question that Morris killed Jim for the reward.

Jim Reed's murder was the great sorrow of Belle's life, but she reacted more with rage and a thirst for vengeance than with grief. She certainly got even with John Morris.

Morris could not get the reward without proving that the man he had killed was Jim Reed, so Belle was summoned to identify the body. The weather was hot, no undertakers were available, and Belle knew that Jim would have to be buried soon. She also knew that no one in the community would admit that they knew the notorious outlaw. The identification that Morris needed could only come from her.

She looked at her husband's bullet-riddled body and then at Morris. Her lips curled in cold hate and scorn. "This sonofabitch Morris," she said, "appears to have murdered the wrong man. If anybody gets the reward for killing Jim Reed, they'll have to kill Jim Reed. This isn't him." Belle turned and rode away without another word. Jim Reed was buried in an unmarked grave, and John Morris did not get the reward.

Belle's vengeance even extended to Jim's own family. She always blamed Jim's brother Solly for not hunting Morris down and killing him.

After her husband's death, Belle moved back to Scyene. Her father died shortly after, and her mother moved away. Belle tried to train Rosie Lee as a dancer, and she appeared once on a stage in Dallas when she was fourteen, but the girl had a nervous disorder and fainted easily. Edward, too, was in poor health.

In 1876 Belle was running a livery stable near Dallas. Besides her influential friends in Dallas, she knew many of her husband's outlaw friends. Soon she was dealing in stolen horses and described by Emmett Dalton, Cole Younger's cousin, as a "fence for horse thieves." Belle's granddaughter, Rosie Lee's daughter Flossie Doe, wrote about her grandmother, explaining that "stealing from a damned Yankee or a carpetbagger was different from stealing from a Texan, and Myra Reed never stole a horse from a Texan."

Flossie Doe's middle name was well chosen. Her mother, then known as Pearl Younger, never revealed the name of the girl's father. Perhaps she didn't know.

Belle's neighbors had never paid attention to her long rides on horseback, sometimes for a week at a time. They assumed she was meeting Jim in some secret hideout. But now they began gossiping about Belle's morals. Being faithful to an outlaw husband was one thing; consorting with outlaws to whom she was not married was another. Belle's friends dropped her away, and she was no longer welcome in respectable Dallas homes.

In 1878 Belle was jailed in Dallas for possession of stolen horses. After about a week, a deputy sheriff let her out, and they disappeared together. A month later he was back with his wife. He claimed that Belle had grabbed his pistol and forced him to let her out. Then she kept him busy cutting wood, carrying water, and doing all the camp cooking. He made his escape from her only by great watchfulness and ingenuity. At least that's what he told his wife.

The incident demonstrates Belle Reed's ability to dominate men. From this point on, most of her outlaw career was played out in Kansas and Indian Territory, although she returned to Texas from time to time. She apparently selected and discarded lovers at will, never finding one to replace the outlaw with whom she first fell in love.

Her lovers—a few of them husbands—included Sam Starr, Blue Duck, John Middleton, Jim July, Jack Spaniard, Jim French, and Bruce Younger, Cole Younger's cousin. All but Patterson, a wealthy Texas rancher, were outlaws. All were outlaws, and all except Bruce Younger died violent deaths, most shot to death by lawmen.

Since Bruce Younger was one of Belle's husbands, it is possible that Pearl Younger got her name from her stepfather and not from a casual acquaintance between her mother and a famous outlaw.

In 1883 Belle became the first woman tried in the courtroom of Isaac Parker, the celebrated "hanging judge" of Fort Smith, Arkansas. The jury found Belle guilty of two counts of stealing horses. Although the judge had already sent eighty-eight men to the gallows, he was unexpectedly lenient, giving Belle six months in a federal prison.

On February 2, 1889, two days before her forty-first birthday, Belle was shot by a bushwhacker as she rode her horse about a mile from her home in Indian Territory. He shot Belle in the back with a shotgun and then, to make sure she was dead, shot her in the face with a pistol. The crime was never solved.

Rosie Lee had the following carved on her mother's grave marker:

> SHED NOT FOR HER THE BITTER TEAR,
> NOR GIVE THE HEART TO VAIN REGRET.
> 'TIS BUT THE CASKET THAT LIES HERE,
> THE GEM THAT FILLS IT SPARKLES YET.

About a year before, while being interviewed by a newspaper reporter, Belle provided what might have been a better inscription when she said, "I regard myself as a woman who has seen much of life."

Two Cities Give Up
the Wild West

Austin, the state capital, and San Antonio, home of the Alamo only eighty miles away, were poised for a change in the mid-1880s. Railroad construction inward from the Gulf of Mexico and downward from the American middle west—and practically all other commerce and industry—had stopped with the Civil War. The readmission of Texas to the Union in 1870 led to a spurt in commerce and a heavy influx of immigrants.

A shoot-out in a San Antonio theater on March 11, 1884, was the catalyst that transformed the two cities from the old Wild West into a tamer, more civilized version of society, a change that would gradually spread outward to the rest of the state. It started when King Fisher suggested to Ben Thompson that they see a vaudeville show in San Antonio. Both were accomplished gunmen, sometimes on one side of the law, sometimes on the other. They weren't even close friends, but they went together to see the show.

Thompson's parents had come from their native Nova Scotia to settle near relatives in Austin in 1851 when Ben was eight. After wounding a friend with a shotgun when he was thirteen and killing an Indian three years later, Ben Thompson went to New Orleans where he killed a Frenchman in a duel. Five feet, nine inches tall, with black hair and blue eyes, Thompson joined the Texas Rangers to fight Juan

Cortina and followed that with Civil War service in the Second Texas Cavalry. After some battles in Texas he returned to the Rangers to patrol along the Rio Grande. Captured by Union officers, he escaped and fled to Mexico to serve in Emperor Maximilian's forces as they tried to restore monarchy to Mexico.

Thompson returned to Texas after the Civil War and operated a gambling saloon in Austin. Acquitted of one killing, he served two years in the state prison for another and then went to Kansas, where he ran afoul of Wild Bill Hickok. He continued his shooting career in Texas and Kansas and eventually returned to Austin to open another gambling saloon. He ran twice for city marshal, losing in 1879 and winning in 1881. Crime dropped to an all-time low during his term in office. During those two years Austin had no murders, burglaries, or assaults with intent to kill.

John King Fisher, eleven years younger than Thompson, was born in Upshur County, Texas, in 1854. Handsome, just under six feet tall with black hair and dark eyes, he was popular with girls. He served a short state prison sentence for burglary when he was sixteen, and then went to Dimmit County, in a rough part of south Texas near the Rio Grande. He became a skilled gunman and the leader of a gang whose territory included several counties around Eagle Pass, his headquarters. He married a childhood sweetheart in 1876.

By 1878, Fisher claimed to have killed seven men, not counting Mexicans. He and a companion were reported to have killed eight Mexicans in a single fight.

Fisher became deputy sheriff of Uvalde County and would run unopposed for sheriff in 1884.

The immediate cause of the 1884 shoot-out in the San Antonio theater was Thompson's earlier killing of Jack Harris on July 11, 1882, in the same theater.

Harris, a Connecticut native, ran away to sea at age twelve. In 1855 he joined William Walker's filibustering expedition to Nicaragua. Captured by one of the political factions struggling for control of the country, he was about to be executed when a rescue party saved him. He came to San Antonio and joined the police force. After Civil War service in the Second Texas Cavalry, he returned to San Antonio, opening a saloon on Market Street.

Harris became a part owner of the Harris Variety Theatre, which opened in 1879 as part of the Vaudeville Theatre and Gambling Saloon on the Main Plaza. His associates in the theater were Joe Foster and Billy Simms, a native of Austin. Ben Thompson had taught Simms to play cards and at one time had him as a partner in his Austin gambling room. Then their friendship turned sour, and Billy moved to San Antonio.

On Monday, July 10, 1882, Thompson took the evening train to San Antonio, hoping to arrest a wanted man. The next afternoon, he went to the Vaudeville Theatre and Gambling Saloon, thinking it the most likely hideout for the man. Thompson and Harris had been feuding for nearly two years. Their falling-out started after a card game, and Harris swore that Thompson would never enter his place of business again. Thompson remained in the gambling room for a short time on July 10 and then quietly left.

The next evening Thompson returned to the Vaudeville Saloon. "You tell Joe Foster that he is a thief," Thompson said to the bartender, "and Jack Harris lives off the labors of the Variety women."

Ben Thompson, Austin, Texas, circa 1882. *Texas State Library and Archives Commission*

"If you want them to hear that, you tell them yourself," the bartender replied.

One of the employees went to Harris's home and told him what Thompson had said. Other employees stationed themselves on watch.

When Harris reached the theater, he armed himself with a shotgun and took a position in the dark where he could see outside to the street. Most of the employees left. Thompson, standing outside, saw the employees leaving, and he stepped forward where he could see Harris through the Venetian blinds.

"What are you doing with that shotgun?" Thompson called out.

"Come on, I'm ready for you," Harris replied.

Harris thought Thompson would enter the building, and he raised his gun to be ready. Thompson drew his pistol, and fired through the Venetian blinds. His bullet ricocheted along a wall and hit Harris, who staggered upstairs where three of his female employees tried to make him comfortable. A doctor came from a drugstore, and Harris was carried home on a stretcher. Thompson's bullet had passed through his lung, cutting several large blood vessels.

Before he died, Harris said, "He took advantage of me and shot me from the dark."

Thompson surrendered the next morning and waited for his trial in the Bat Cave, the name given to San Antonio's original jail and courthouse. The lawyers for the prosecution and defense included the most prominent barristers in Austin and San Antonio. After many months and many motions, the trial began on January 16, 1883. Long before that, Thompson had tendered his resignation as city marshal (chief of police) to the Austin city council. The council refused to accept it, giving Thompson a sixty-day leave of absence, instead.

On the fourth day of trial, the jury acquitted Thompson. By then his term had ended, so his enthusiastic welcome back in Austin became his last acclaim from a grateful public.

Thompson, former outlaw and state prison inmate, was much admired in Austin for the dramatic drop in violent crime. So was King Fisher in Uvalde, where he had been acting sheriff before being elected to the position. As the leader of gunmen farther south, he had once posted a sign at an intersection: "This is King Fisher's road. Take the other one." At one time an entire company of Rangers was occupied in trying to break up the King Fisher gang. Uvalde citizens liked Fisher's direct way of running gunmen out. Children stared in awe as he walked the streets, and admiring citizens gathered around whenever he stopped.

On March 11, 1884, Fisher went to Austin to learn about a new law making fence-cutting a felony. When he finished his business, he called on the former city marshal. Thompson's behavior had changed after the tumultuous reception he received following his acquittal of murdering Jack Harris. No longer city marshal, he became increasingly irritable, drank more, and had trouble sleeping. He used his pistol once to force a bartender into serving Negroes in the portion of a bar reserved for whites, then apologized and went outside to shoot up the organ of an itinerant organ grinder. Another time he "staggered" into a crowded theater and began shooting his pistol wildly in the crowd. He was soon alone in the theater, but it was only Thompson's way of having fun—all his cartridges were blanks!

King Fisher's calling on Thompson before he returned to Uvalde may have been part of an effort to reconcile their differences. Jack Harris had been Fisher's friend, and he resented Thompson's killing of the man. Thompson agreed to board the train with King Fisher and ride until it met the northbound train, but they began drinking and he continued on to San Antonio. Thompson had no intention of visiting the Vaudeville Theatre. In fact, he told Fisher that Joe Foster had invited him back and he had no intention of going.

"They won't catch me in that trap," he told Fisher. "I know if I were to go into that place it would be my graveyard."

When they reached San Antonio at eight o'clock, they both got off the train. In the meantime someone on the train had sent a telegram ahead warning Simms that the men were coming. Afterward it was claimed that the police had suggested that Thompson be shot upon the slightest provocation.

The two men had supper, attended a play in another theater, and then went to the theater where Thompson had killed Jack Harris two years before. Probably no other gunplay in Texas has been witnessed by so many people or been described in so many conflicting accounts. Thompson and Fisher stopped in the bar long enough for Thompson to ask that Simms be sent to him. Fisher had long been fond of Joe Foster, the other owner of the theater. Possibly he was trying to work a reconciliation between Simms and Thompson, who had once been friends in Austin.

But it was not a night for reconciliation. Thompson bought tickets for the vaudeville performance, and he and Fisher went to the balcony where they could buy drinks while watching the performance. There they talked to Simms and a policeman named Coy. Then Thompson saw Joe Foster and invited him over for a drink. Foster refused the drink and also refused to shake hands with the man who had killed his friend.

"I don't want no trouble," Foster said. "Just leave me alone."

Simms and Coy both testified afterward that Thompson whipped out his pistol and rammed it into Foster's mouth. Then Coy said he grabbed the gun and held the cylinder as best he could, and that a bullet whizzed past his ear.

Guns roared, and Thompson, Fisher, and Coy fell in a heap. Thompson and Fisher were dead, and Foster had a leg wound that soon killed him. A coroner's inquest found that Coy and Foster had killed the men to save their own lives, but old-timers, some of them witnesses, called it an ambush.

Austin newspapers raged with indignation. An autopsy performed in the capital city found that eight shots had struck Thompson. Five of those had entered his head, supporting the statements of witnesses that a group of armed men sat in balcony boxes above Thompson and Fisher. For that matter, it was clear that the five bullets had all entered *at the same angle*, as if it had been a planned execution by a firing squad, all shooting in unison.

Austin newspapers made much of the fact that the San Antonio coroner's jury reported only three wounds in Thompson. But eventually Austin citizens came to realize that Ben Thompson had turned from a nuisance into a menace. Perhaps on that fateful evening he wanted to make up with Simms and Foster. We will never know.

What we do know is that Austin and San Antonio citizens realized that the time of the frontier gunslinger had ended. No longer could the good traits that men appreciated in their friends—courage, loyalty, humor—excuse brutality and selfishness, bad traits showing up in the same men. People noticed that two of the men killed in the execution were good friends, and one of them had probably ordered the execution. Texas, by mid-1884, was too civilized to continue permitting the wanton gunslinging of the frontier, and that awareness came to both Austin and San Antonio on that one violent night in March 1884.

The March 13 *San Antonio Daily Express* summed up the community feeling: "There seems to be little concern among the people as to who did it. That it was done, and well done, seems satisfactory enough. The two great desperadoes are dead, the last of their kind among us we hope, and the whole state should mark the occasion with a white stone."

Two Friends
in the Hoo Doo War

On August 10, 1875, Johann Wohrle and Charles Harcourt rested from their work cleaning a well in Mason County, Texas. The burning sun, high in the summer sky, beat down without mercy. Wohrle had recently and very suddenly resigned as deputy sheriff of Mason County to take up the work of a handyman. He had hired Harcourt, his old buddy from B Company of the Third US Cavalry, to help on the well cleaning job. As they reminisced about Civil War service in the Yankee cavalry, Scott Cooley rode up.

Cooley, a short, solid man who claimed to be half Cherokee, had lived in Jack County during the Comanche and Kiowa raids. By the time he was nineteen he had become a ruthless Indian fighter. Later he served with the Texas Rangers. One time he killed a wounded Indian in an attack, skinned the hide off his back, and said he would make a quirt from it.

Wohrle and Harcourt, leaning back against an old slab and wire fence that had been part of a hog pen in its better days, watched as Cooley dismounted, tied his horse to a mesquite bush, and approached.

"Reckon a feller can get a drink here?" Cooley asked.

"Not from that well," Wohrle replied. "It's mostly mud. We're cleaning it."

Harcourt shrugged a shoulder toward a burlap-wrapped earthenware jug nearby. The burlap was dry except for a narrow rim of moisture at the jug's mouth. "You're welcome to our jug," he said. "Ain't quite as warm yet as panther piss."

After exchanging a few pleasantries, Harcourt and Wohrle got to their feet. "Time we was getting back to work," Wohrle said.

Cooley walked with them to the well and watched as Wohrle held the windlass while Harcourt climbed into the well bucket.

Wohrle let the windlass turn to lower the bucket into the well. As Harcourt's head dropped below ground level, he heard Cooley ask in a soft voice, "Wohrle, why did you kill Williamson?"

"Because I had to."

"Then I reckon that's why I'm killing you."

Cooley shot Wohrle dead, and Harcourt barely survived the twenty-five-foot fall to the well bottom. Cooley fired six more shots into Wohrle's dead body, stabbed it four times, scalped it, stuffed the dripping scalp into his pocket, and rode away.

Ethnic wars produce more violence than those fought over ideology. The Mason County War in the 1870s was a good example. It pitted recent German immigrants against Americans who had been in Texas longer, and some of its embers of hate still glowed thirty years later. Sometimes they called it the Hoo Doo War, a term whose meaning has been lost but was more accurate since the war also included Llano County.

The rugged Hill Country west of Austin was a harsh land, and it produced hard men. The saga of murder began when German farmers and stockmen adopted vigilante methods to protect themselves from what they called American outlaws. Very likely some of the "outlaws" were drovers using long ropes and fast horses to get a start in ranching, tactics that had been used elsewhere in Texas and the West for decades. Others

Portrait of John Ringo. *Courtesy of the Arizona Historical Society, Tucson, AHS #78486*

were probably completely innocent of any wrongdoing, but the Germans, generally called the Mob, never gave the law a chance to make that determination.

Most of the men involved were good and honest men, but good men sometimes make bad decisions. The Hoo Doo War serves as a fine example of how ethnic hatred eventually destroys those whom it infects.

On April 9, 1874, Mason County Sheriff John Clark, leading a posse of German settlers (members of the Mob), arrested eleven drovers in Llano County, which bordered Mason County on the east. The drovers claimed that they were gathering their own cattle and that Clark had no authority in Llano County. The latter statement was, of course, true.

Two drovers were immediately released, and three more had their charges dropped in return for their testimony. After a six-hour trial the next day, a Llano County jury found the others guilty, and the judge fined them $2,500. They retaliated by charging Clark and his entire posse with robbery and false imprisonment.

Opposing camps hurled charges back and forth. The Llano County sheriff tried repeatedly to serve his papers on Clark to appear in Llano County and answer to the new charges, but could not find him.

In February 1875, Sheriff Clark struck again! He arrested cattlemen in McCulloch County, bordering Mason County on the north, for cattle theft. Now events progressed so quickly that these men would never be brought to trial.

Near midnight on February 18, some of the Mob broke into the home of Johann Wohrle, one of Clark's deputies, and demanded the keys to the Mason County jail where the

McCulloch County cattlemen were confined. When Wohrle refused their demand, they tortured him by strangulation while his pregnant wife watched, screaming in hysterics. The deputy finally turned over the keys, and the attackers headed for the jail.

Sheriff Clark poked a rifle out a courthouse window and shouted that he would shoot anyone who tried to enter the jail. Ten men from the Mob talked privately with Clark, who then left, saying he was going for help. The Mob opened the jail and took out five prisoners.

The attempt to hang all five prisoners was thwarted when armed citizens, led by a few Texas Rangers, showed up and started shooting. Two men were hanged, and one was shot to death. Another was cut down before he died, and the fifth escaped.

The *San Antonio Herald* reported with some irony:

> Instead of five men being hung, only two were hung and one was shot. For the sake of the reputation of Mason as a law abiding community we hope this correction will be made.

Mrs. Wohrle miscarried a few days after her night of horror.

The Texas Rangers did nothing to bring the vigilantes to justice for the lynching. The Mob could only interpret this as approval of what they had done. Within three weeks of the February lynching, the Mob had killed three more men.

One of Sheriff Clark's duties was the collection of taxes. He got into a dispute with Tim Williamson, a prominent cattleman in Mason County, about what Williamson owed, and Williamson wanted to fight Clark about it. Clark refused to fight, but had his deputy, Wohrle, arrest Williamson for cattle theft. While Wohrle was bringing Williamson to Mason to put him in jail on May 13, 1875, a band of ten or fifteen men, their faces blackened, attacked. Williamson begged Wohrle to let him make a run for it. Instead, Wohrle shot Williamson's horse, and left him standing alone to face the onrushing Mob, which killed him. The facts clearly showed that the ambush had been prearranged.

Williamson's murder changed the Hoo Doo War from a dispute about the control of cattle to a war of vengeance that would rage through Mason and Llano Counties. Williamson's best friend was Scott Cooley, who broke down and cried when he learned of his friend's killing.

Williamson and his wife had taken Cooley in as a boy and raised him like their own. Once, Mrs. Williamson nursed him back to life after he contracted typhoid. Cooley had made two trail drives to Kansas with Williamson; now he swore revenge against all connected with Williamson's death.

The ethnic nature of the Hoo Doo War clouded the facts. Certainly Deputy Wohrle was a faithful officer when he refused to give up the jail keys until after he was tortured and his wife suffered a miscarriage. But some wondered if Wohrle's loyalty had shifted to the Mob when he later failed to oppose the killing of Williamson. Scott Cooley's close friendship with Williamson overcame all doubts for him. He reasoned that either or both Clark and Wohrle had arranged for the ambush that killed his friend.

Cooley farmed in Menardville to the west of Mason County, and was completely unknown in the town of Mason. He went there immediately, stayed several days, and kept his ears open. Soon he knew the names of the men in the Mob who had killed Williamson. Wohrle's sudden resignation as deputy sheriff to become a handyman convinced Cooley even more that his friend's killer was in complete sympathy with the Mob.

About a week after Cooley caught up with Wohrle at the well, he killed and scalped Karl Bader, another member of the Mob, at Bader's home in Llano County.

Now it was clear to the Mob that someone had a hit list of the vigilantes who had killed Williamson. The *Austin Daily Statesman* reported:

> No arrests have been made, and every man about
> Mason is afraid to open his mouth one way or the other.
> Neighbors are afraid of each other, and will not travel the
> road in company with any man. [The Texas Rangers]
> may succeed in restoring quietness, but the apprehension
> is that the worst has not come.

Cooley summoned another close friend, John Ringo, to help him get even. Ringo, a tall (six feet, two inches), handsome man with strong, somber features, dark hair, and ice-blue eyes, spoke softly like a gentleman. He reflected good breeding and a cultured background.

In 1864, when Ringo was fourteen, his family traveled from Missouri in a wagon train to California. In Wyoming, his father accidentally killed himself with his own shotgun while standing guard against Indians. Mrs. Ringo and the five children settled in San Jose near her sister whose husband was Coleman Younger, uncle of the outlaw Younger brothers. Ringo was also connected by marriage to the family of Jesse and Frank James, with whom the Youngers often rode.

Ringo was an intelligent man and an avid reader. He was also a crack shot by the time he was twelve. Ringo left California in the early 1870s. On Christmas Day 1874, he was charged with unlawfully discharging a pistol in Burnet, Texas. By then he was a close friend with Scott Cooley, the former Texas Ranger.

In early September 1875, the Mob paid Jim Cheyney to ride to Loyal Valley and entice Mose Beard and George Gladden, supporters of Cooley, to ride to Mason. About halfway to Mason, Sheriff Clark and about sixty men ambushed them, killing Beard and wounding Gladden. Gladden also would have been killed, but a member of the Mob suddenly changed his mind and insisted that they had done enough. Another member cut Beard's finger off to get a ring he wore.

By now many men from both Llano and Burnet Counties, besides Ringo, had reached Mason County to help Scott Cooley. Citizens in Mason County, fearing a civil war, begged the governor to return the Rangers to their county. Forty Rangers were promptly dispatched.

Many of the Rangers sympathized with Cooley, with whom they had served. They didn't look very hard for their man, and rumors spread that some Rangers were meeting Cooley at night and telling him that they didn't care if he killed every "Dutchman" (German) in the county who was a member of the Mob.

Major John Jones called his Frontier Battalion of Rangers together, told them how proud he was of their service, and continued:

> I personally feel kindly toward every man in the Ranger service. I know some of you feel that way toward Scott Cooley, but you have taken an oath to protect the state

of Texas against all enemies. Tim Williamson met a horrible death at the hands of a relentless mob, but that did not justify Cooley in killing people in a private war of vengeance in defiance of the law and the Rangers.

Now, men, I have a proposition for you. If every man who sympathizes with Scott Cooley and his gang and does not wish to pursue him to the bitter end will step out of ranks, I will issue him an honorable discharge and let him quit the service clean.

Fifteen men stepped forward, and the major continued. "Now I expect all the rest of you to use all diligence and strength in breaking up and capturing these violators of the law."

Mose Beard had been a popular man in Mason County. The Cooley gang was determined to get even with the man who had lured him to his death. On September 25, John Ringo and one other man rode up to Cheyney's house in Mason, where Cheyney was cooking breakfast for his family. Without warning, they shot and killed Cheyney in the presence of his family. Then they rode to the hotel and joined Cooley and Gladden and others of Cooley's friends to have their breakfast. They boasted publicly that they "had made beef out of Cheyney and if someone did not bury him, he would stink."

Four days later Cooley, John Baird, and several others (probably not including Ringo) ambushed Dan Hoerster and two others on the street in Mason, killing Hoerster. Hoerster had been brand inspector for Mason County. He and Clark were the main county officials who supported the Mob. Shortly after he had led the early-September ambush that killed Mose Beard and wounded George Gladden, Sheriff Clark disappeared from Mason County and was not again heard from until long after the Hoo Doo War ended.

At the end of December 1875, Cooley and Ringo were arrested for threatening the lives of the Burnet County sheriff and his deputy. Fearing that Cooley and Ringo's friends would help them escape custody, the authorities took their prisoners to Austin and jailed them there. Their trial was moved to Lampasas County, where they were found guilty in March 1876.

In May, while their conviction was on appeal and with the help of outsiders, Cooley and Ringo escaped from the Lampasas County jail. An attempt in July to free other men from the Lampasas jail was thought to be led by Ringo.

On October 31, 1876, Rangers captured Ringo and George Gladden and brought them to the Travis County jail. There Ringo met John Wesley Hardin, also an inmate of the jail. In fact Hardin complained about being confined in the same jail with such a vicious prisoner as Ringo.

By this time Cooley had returned to Blanco County, where he had lived before. There he died (probably in June 1876), either from a brain infection or from poison. Probably psychotic, Cooley had continued to carry Wohrle's scalp in his pocket, often exhibiting it to impress people.

The next month the grand jury of Mason County indicted Ringo, Gladden, and others for the murder of James Cheyney. Ringo's conviction for threatening the Burnet County sheriff was reversed, but he was immediately rearrested on the new warrant from Mason County.

On January 21, 1877, the Mason County courthouse burned, destroying all records of the Hoo Doo War.

In May 1878, the Mason County case was dismissed against Ringo because no witnesses to testify against him could be found. Gladden was convicted and sentenced to ninety-nine years. For a brief time Ringo served as a constable in Loyal Valley; then he moved on west, showing up in Arizona by December 1879. On December 14, 1879, he wounded another man in a Tombstone saloon shoot-out.

After the OK Corral gunfight in Tombstone on October 26, 1881, Ringo became the leader of the anti-Earp forces. On January 17, 1882, he challenged Doc Holliday to a street fight. Both men were armed, but Holliday declined. John Pleasant Gray, a rancher who knew all the parties, said that Ringo found Wyatt Earp in front of the Crystal Palace Saloon and also challenged him. Ringo pulled off his neckerchief, flipped it toward Earp, and told him to take the other end and say when. Gray wrote, "Of course Wyatt Earp was too wise to be caught in such a trap."

On July 14, 1882, John Ringo was found dead on Turkey Creek in the foothills of the Chiricahua Mountains by a teamster hauling wood. His death became the ultimate mystery in a consistently mysterious life.

Ringo had been on a long drinking binge and was found in a grove of oaks with his revolver clenched in his right hand. People called it suicide, but there were disturbing factors: Ringo's boots were off, and his feet were wrapped in strips of an undershirt. It appeared that he had traveled a short distance in that footwear. His horse was found some time later, still saddled. Ringo's body was in a sitting position, the back against a tree. His right temple had a bullet hole, the bullet coming out the top of the left side of his head. Part of the scalp that was missing appeared to have been cut by a knife.

His rifle leaned against a nearby tree. He wore two cartridge belts; the belt with the revolver cartridges was buckled on upside down. His six-shot revolver had five cartridges in it. One writer claimed that it had not been fired, but the coroner's jury just noted that the revolver had the five cartridges. It said nothing about whether the sixth chamber had an empty casing. If it had no empty casing, it would have been impossible for Ringo to have extracted it after the top of his head was blown off.

Former sheriff John Clark had fled for safety to Ripley County in a remote area of southeastern Missouri. Clark knew the county, having served as a deputy sheriff there before the Civil War. It was a land of rugged hills, caves, and tight little valleys through which wild rivers ran rampant. Clark bought a farm in the most inaccessible part of the county, fearing until the end of his life that the relentless Scott Cooley would find him and kill him.

There Clark lived like a recluse, dying on May 8, 1888. He may not have known that Ringo died six years before, and Cooley six years before that. Probably such knowledge would have made no difference. Ex-sheriff Clark knew that others besides the two friends would have welcomed the chance to kill him.

Border Bandits

J. Frank Dobie, Walter Prescott Webb, and other historians estimated that Mexicans stole nine hundred thousand head of Texas cattle during the twenty-five years from 1850 to 1875. *Huero* (red-complexioned Spaniard) Juan Nepomuceno Cortina was supreme chieftain of the hundreds of Mexican cattle thieves during their long scourge on the border. They did, however, leave enough cattle that the region between the Nueces River and the Rio Grande became the incubator for the range cattle industry in America.

Cortina, born May 16, 1824, in Camargo, Tamaulipas, had an uneducated, undistinguished *ranchero* father, but his mother's family was as renowned as any that Spain sent to the New World. Juan, the black sheep of the family, never learned to read and only learned to sign his name after he proclaimed himself governor of Tamaulipas.

As a lieutenant in the Mexican Army, Cortina resisted the American invasion of 1846. After the war, the army caught him stealing horses from his own government and discharged him. He took civilian employment and then murdered his employer for some unknown reason.

Cortina's mother owned most of the land surrounding Brownsville and Matamoros on both sides of the Rio Grande. Making his headquarters on the American side, Cortina claimed that all the cattle in the area belonged to him as descendants from his grandmother's original herd. He began paying fifty cents per head for all cattle delivered to him in the free trade zone on the Mexican side of the river. He soon had three thousand men "licensed" to deliver cattle. He warned the men that if they stole on the Mexican side, he would see them hanged; if on the American side, he would see them protected.

Called by some the Red Robber of the Rio Grande, Cortina made an impressive appearance as he rode into Brownsville each morning for coffee. His fair complexion, brown hair, grayish-green eyes, and reddish beard set him apart from his people. He inherited personal charm and excellent manners from his mother, and he had become fearless, self-possessed, and cunning. A strong, muscular man of medium height, he had leadership flair, a gambler's disposition, and a good intuition about the character of his followers.

The simmering difficulties of Texas ranchers over the growing loss of their cattle to Mexico broke into open war on July 3, 1859. That morning, while Cortina drank his coffee, he saw a Brownsville city marshal arrest a drunken Mexican who had formerly worked for Cortina. The marshal's conduct seemed unnecessarily harsh, and Cortina remonstrated, mildly at first. Upset at the interference, the marshal answered with an insult, and Cortina shot him in the shoulder. Then he galloped out of town in grand style, the rescued man seated on his horse behind him.

No one knows exactly where Cortina spent the following two months, but rumors kept circulating about mounted men gathering on both sides of the river for some kind of military action. After all, the nation that a dozen or so years before had, with questionable right, invaded Mexico now had seen one of its own law officers shot while making an arrest in an American city. What would the Yankees do now? Cooler heads tried to get Cortina out of Texas, but they couldn't find him.

Before daylight on September 28, Brownsville residents heard the gallop of horses and shouts in the streets—*Vivan Cortinas! Mueran los Gringos* (Kill the Yankees)! *Viva la República de México!* By dawn Cortina and a hundred men had captured Brownsville. Cortina wanted to kill the sheriff, but the man escaped. Cortina's men did kill three Americans, whom he described as "wicked men." They also broke into the jail, killed the jailer, and freed about a dozen prisoners. Major Samuel P. Heintzelman, who had recently commanded American troops in south Texas, reported to Colonel Robert E. Lee that an American city of almost three thousand people was occupied by armed bandits, a calamity previously unheard of in the United States.

In his first proclamation Cortina said they would not hurt the innocent but would strike for the emancipation of the Mexicans. He added "our personal enemies shall not possess our land until they have fattened it with their own gore."

Brownsville residents appealed to Mexican soldiers under General Caravajal to protect them. So for a time Mexican soldiers quartered in a US fort—Fort Brown had been evacuated some months before by the United States Army—were protecting Americans on American soil from Mexican bandits under the command of a man who claimed—falsely, as he was born just south of the Rio Grande—that he was an American citizen.

For the next two and a half months Cortina's men faced both Americans and other Mexicans protecting Americans in skirmishes, most of which the Cortina forces won. By early December, Cortina had become a great conqueror, and Texans feared that he might force the international boundary back to the Nueces River, 130 miles to the north. The Mexican flag flew over Cortina's headquarters, and men flocked to join him.

On December 14, regular army troops under Major Heintzelman, assisted by Texas Rangers, engaged the Cortina forces. In a series of skirmishes the army and Rangers forced Cortina to retreat about a hundred miles up the river to Rio Grande City, where he crossed into Mexico, and the Cortina occupation of south Texas ended.

An occasional cross-border raid into Texas continued to remind ranchers that the bandit Cortina was still alive and well. He was indicted for stealing cattle at least twice by the Cameron County grand jury, but they could never find him to prosecute.

In February 1860, Cortina showed up at La Bolsa, apparently planning to capture the steamboat *Ranchero*, owned by Richard King and Mifflin Kenedy, who were raising cattle on their King Ranch, a hundred miles northeast. John Ford's Texas Rangers crossed the Rio Grande and chased Cortina away.

The next month Colonel Robert E. Lee, then commanding the Eighth Military Department in San Antonio, got orders to demand that Mexico break up Cortina's bands. If the authorities refused, Lee was authorized to pursue Cortina's troops into Mexico. Lee led troops to the lower Rio Grande Valley but could not find Cortina. He did return with the promise of Mexican officials that they would try to find Cortina and arrest him.

In May 1861, when Texas seceded from the Union, Cortina invaded Zapata County and attacked the county seat. Santos Benavides, a captain in the Confederate Army, drove Cortina back into Mexico. Throughout the Civil War, Cortina continued to steal cattle in Texas. When General E. O. C. Ord began investigating lawlessness on the Rio Grande frontier, the

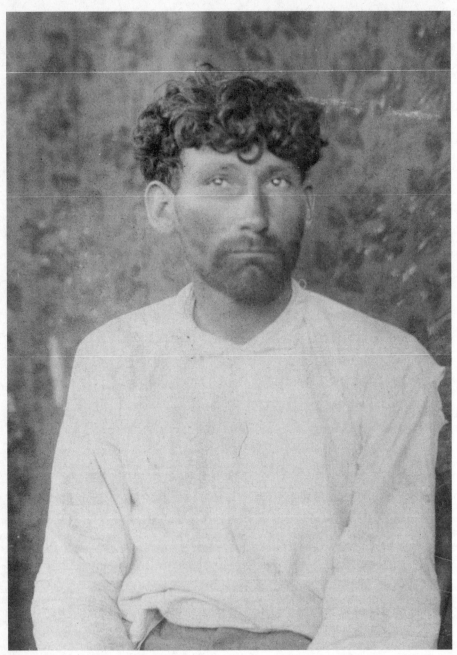

Photograph of Gregorio Cortez. *Texas State Library and Archives Commission*

Mexican government became concerned and took Cortina into custody in July 1875. He was paroled to Mexico City and never again allowed to hold power in Mexico.

Cortina died on October 30, 1894, and was buried in Mexico City with full military honors.

In July 1875, when the Mexican authorities isolated Cortina in Mexico City, Rosalie Lira Cortina and her husband, Ramón Cortez Garza, had just christened their son, born on June 22, Gregorio Cortez Lira. The parents were transient laborers, then living near Matamoros. We don't know if Gregorio was a grandson of Juan Cortina, but he grew up to take Cortina's place in the legends of border banditry.

Gregorio's parents moved to Manor, just outside Austin, when the boy was twelve. From ages fourteen to twenty-four, Gregorio and his brother Romaldo worked as seasonal farm hands and *vaqueros* in Karnes, Gonzales, and neighboring counties.

Gregorio, standing five feet nine inches tall and weighing 145 pounds, was small but wiry. His shoulders stooped slightly, and his jet-black hair tumbled in heavy curls, partially hiding his long, aquiline face. He talked without affection and took pains to make himself clear, often repeating statements to be sure he was understood.

Gregorio married Leonor Diaz, and their first child was born when Gregorio was sixteen. Gregorio and Romaldo, married but childless, took their families with them as they followed the seasonal work.

In 1900 the Cortez brothers settled down on rented land in Karnes County to farm for themselves. On June 12, 1901, Gregorio and Romaldo had just finished their noon meal and were resting on the front porch of Gregorio's house. Gregorio lay full length on the floor, his head in Leonor's lap. Gregorio's mother and Romaldo and his wife sat nearby. Gregorio's children were inside, eating their meal. The day was hot and clear, and the brothers' tall corn promised a good harvest for their first year as independent farmers.

Thirty-one-year-old W. T. (Brack) Morris, serving his third term as Karnes County sheriff, rode up with one of his deputies, Boone Choate, supposedly an expert in Spanish. Morris was looking for a horse thief wanted in Atascosa County. The only description he had was "a medium-sized Mexican with a big, red, Mexican hat." Morris had talked to Mexicans in Kenedy and learned that one of them had recently acquired a mare in a trade with Gregorio Cortez. Later investigation would reveal that Gregorio had the mare legally, and that the Kenedy informant knew the mare's history when he talked to Morris.

Romaldo greeted the lawmen at the gate and then returned to the house to say to Gregorio, *"Te quieren,"* which literally means, "you are wanted," but was a common way of saying, "someone wants to talk to you." Choate thought that both brothers knew that Gregorio was a wanted man, and he probably told that to Morris.

When Gregorio came out to the front fence, Choate asked if he had traded a *caballo* (horse—the correct term in agricultural communities for the male equine) to the informant. Apparently Choate could not think of *yegua*, the word for mare. Gregorio answered truthfully, "No."

Sheriff Morris got out of his buggy, and told Choate to tell the brothers that he was going to arrest them. Choate interpreted Gregorio's response as "No white man can arrest me." It appeared later at Gregorio's trial that he had said, "You can't arrest me for nothing." Gregorio had never been in trouble or arrested before. Apparently Choate had misunderstood another Spanish word.

Romaldo, unarmed, stood about twelve feet away, listening and watching. Morris suddenly drew his weapon, shot Romaldo in the face, and fired at Gregorio, but missed. There was evidence at the trial that Romaldo was moving toward Morris when he shot him. Gregorio's return shot mortally wounded the sheriff. Choate ran away as fast as he could.

Morris staggered to the gate and collapsed. Gregorio shot him again as he lay on the ground. The family treated Romaldo's wound, loaded him into the sheriff's buggy, and carried him to his own house, while Morris was wandering away in the chaparral, bleeding to death. Gregorio saddled a small sorrel mare for himself and a horse for his brother, and set out for Kenedy to get medical care for Romaldo.

Riding through the brush was difficult because Romaldo, feverish, kept falling off his horse. Finally Gregorio stopped and laid his dying brother under a tree. From mid-afternoon until dark the two lay in the brush less than five miles from Gregorio's home while a posse of at least fifty searched the area. The posse didn't find Morris's body until they stumbled on it the next morning. The posse did find the Cortez family, and they terrified the children, who cowered under the table while the men were in Romaldo's house.

Gregorio had to abandon both animals and carry Romaldo all five miles into Kenedy. It took him from sunset until one o'clock in the morning. He left his brother with a family that he knew could obtain medical aid, and then disappeared into the darkness.

Knowing that his pursuers would expect him to head south to the border, Gregorio struck out on foot to the north. He hoped to reach Gonzales County, hide for a few days, and then move on north to Austin, where he had relatives. It took him forty hours to travel about eighty miles to Gonzales County. He had to travel slowly to avoid the posses that were looking for him.

At sundown on the fourteenth, after those forty hours, Gregorio reached the Schnabel ranch, where he knew he could hide with a friend, Martín Robledo.

Gregorio's wife, mother, and sister-in-law had all been jailed, and Robert M. Glover, Gonzales County sheriff and a good friend of Sheriff Morris, had talked to them and pressured them to tell him where Gregorio planned to hide.

By the time Gregorio came out on Robledo's porch to rest his feet after his harrowing hike, Glover's posse were in the brush behind the house, planning their attack. Present at the house were Robledo; his wife; their three sons, ages eighteen, sixteen, and thirteen; a visitor, Martín Sandoval; and a half-grown boy, Ramón Rodríguez, who lived with the Robledo family.

Glover had four deputies, ranch owner Henry Schnabel, and one Mexican in his posse. There was evidence that the posse had been drinking on their way to the Robledo house. Glover divided the posse into three groups to surround the house and attack from three sides at once. The first shots were exchanged between Glover and Gregorio, and Glover was killed. After that exchange, Robledo, his oldest son, and Sandoval all ran into the brush to hide, as did Gregorio. There was no evidence that any of them, except Gregorio, was armed or fired any shots.

Heavy firing continued, and Henry Schnabel, the rancher, was killed by one of the posse. Mrs. Robledo and the three younger boys, all unarmed, were in the house when the deputies broke in, after the other men had run into the brush. Mrs. Robledo was shot while shielding her sons, and the Rodríguez boy was also wounded.

The officers initially reported that ten rifles were confiscated in the house. By the time of the trial, the evidence showed that only one rifle was in the house, the normal weaponry in country homes at that time. It had not been fired.

After the posse left with Mrs. Robledo and the younger boys under arrest, Gregorio slipped back into the house and got his shoes. This time he headed straight for the Rio Grande. On Saturday morning he reached the Guadalupe River and the home of another friend, Ceferino Flores. In the two and a half days since he had killed Sheriff Morris, he had walked nearly a hundred miles. Flores took Gregorio's pistol and gave him his own, along with his sorrel mare and saddle.

Riding now on the second small sorrel mare in his memorable flight, Gregorio again struck southwest. A posse followed close behind, and it stopped to give Flores the rope treatment—successive "hangings" until he told what he knew. Flores served two years in prison for helping his friend.

Between Saturday morning and Sunday evening, the little sorrel mare carried Gregorio from the Guadalupe to the San Antonio River. It was only fifty miles on the map, but with posses and bloodhounds looking for him, the doubling back and giving of false leads, and sometimes the shooting, Gregorio rode many more.

Shortly after noon Sunday a fresh posse picked up his trail. For six hours Gregorio galloped, circling and zigzagging, with mounted pursuers sometimes as close as five hundred yards behind. About six o'clock the little mare stopped. She could go no farther. Gregorio barely slipped off her back before she fell over, dead.

He took the saddle and bridle and hid in the brush while the closest posse broke into small groups and continued its search. After dark, Gregorio found a little brown mare in a pasture, saddled her, cut the fence, and started on the last segment of his flight.

He passed through Floresville, about a hundred miles from Cotulla. Dodging pursuers constantly, it took him three days and almost three hundred miles of riding to reach Cotulla. The posses had to stop from time to time for fresh horses, and one of them killed at least six horses in the pursuit.

Sometimes Gregorio would collect a small group of cattle and herd them along to hide his tracks. Once, desperate for water, he drove a small group to a water hole and drank in plain sight of armed pursuers, who thought he was a local *vaquero*.

Finally, near Cotulla, the little brown mare could go no farther. Gregorio rode her into a thicket and went ahead on foot. By noon on June 20, the mare had been found and the thicket surrounded. Trying to look like a *vaquero* without a horse, Gregorio walked on through Cotulla. On the evening of June 20, he reached a water tank where he lay down and slept for two nights and a day. He woke on the morning of June 22, his twenty-sixth birthday. Later that day he surrendered, without resistance, to a small group of Texas Rangers.

In the ten days since he had shot Sheriff Morris, Gregorio had crisscrossed seven counties, traveling hundreds of miles—some on the backs of three small mares and some on foot—as he evaded more than a hundred peace officers and their deputized posses. During this long and deadly manhunt at least nine Mexicans had been killed, three more wounded, and seven more arrested.

For the next thirty-four months Gregorio was moved through a succession of county jails as Texas authorities prosecuted him for murdering three persons and stealing a horse. After reversals by the appellate court in Austin, retrials, one hung jury, and one dismissal by a judge, the total number of trials reached eight.

The only defense lawyer who stayed faithful to the end was R. B. Abernathy of Gonzales. It brought him neither money nor popularity, and no one could accuse him of courting Mexican votes. At that time in that part of Texas, Mexicans were not allowed to vote in primaries.

Before Gregorio's first conviction was reversed and while he waited for his second trial, a mob of three hundred to three hundred fifty people tried to take him from the Gonzales County jail and lynch him. Sheriff F. M. Fly, who had succeeded Glover, held the mob off and saved Gregorio's life. Interestingly, the mob did not want him for killing a sheriff (he had already been convicted of one of those crimes), but for killing rancher Schnabel. At that time it was common knowledge that the rancher had been killed by a fellow posseman. Fly said most of the mob was from Karnes County.

Gregorio's long siege of trials ended on January 1, 1905, when he started serving a life sentence for Glover's murder. Abernathy kept working, and twelve years later Governor Oscar B. Colquitt pardoned Gregorio.

When Gregorio walked into freedom at age thirty-eight, he had spent a third of his life in prison, all because he had traded a mare for a stallion and an interpreter didn't know the difference. He died of pneumonia three years later in Anson, Texas, over five hundred miles from the border on which he was born and which he had once tried desperately to reach with the help of three little mares.

Rest and Recuperation in Texas

So far as we know, the West's largest outlaw gang, the Wild Bunch, never committed a crime in Texas. But according to the principal Pinkerton detective who investigated them, Butch Cassidy, the Sundance Kid, and other members of the gang hid out in Texas after every job. Their favorite hideout was Fannie Porter's brothel in San Antonio. Here they found rest, recuperation, and entertainment in a place where no detective or lawman ever thought to look for them.

Fannie Porter's was San Antonio's most famous brothel. There Harry Longabaugh (the Sundance Kid) met the beautiful Etta Place, and Harvey Logan (Kid Curry) met Annie Rogers. Robert LeRoy Parker, a Mormon called Butch Cassidy, was not known to patronize prostitutes elsewhere in the West, but he did enjoy visits to Fannie's. At least two others of Fannie's girls formed relationships—some enduring, others not—with members of the gang.

Fannie Porter, born in New Orleans in 1859, showed up in San Antonio in the late 1870s as a female boarder—census terminology for prostitute—at Mrs. J. G. Murphy's house on Pecan Street. By 1897 Fannie had her own two-story, twelve-room house at 505 South San Saba Street. The 1910 census lists Fannie's house as the residence of five female boarders, aged nineteen to twenty-four.

Etta Place and the Sundance Kid. *Reproduced from the collections of the Library of Congress*

Fannie acquired a long criminal arrest record, but only for vagrancy. Prostitution, always illegal in Texas, was barely frowned upon by the public. The police made occasional arrests of madams to calm the few complainers. They never arrested prostitutes, unless for other crimes such as disturbing the peace, falling down drunk, or shooting someone.

Fannie was an attractive, buxom woman of average height. She was described often as a hard, shrewd woman who made a small fortune hiding out train robbers, outlaws, horse thieves, and killers for a price. She was well-known to the law, but more than once she had chased an officer from her place with a broom. Fannie operated a classy establishment. She had a carpeted parlor, fine glass fixtures, and silk sheets on the beds. Favorite customers were served chilled champagne. Fannie never discouraged her girls from becoming seriously involved with the customers.

Annie Rogers, a pretty Texas girl with red hair, was the favorite of Kid Curry. Curry could be called the founder of the Wild Bunch. He took over leadership of some loosely organized bands of rustlers and added bank and train robbery to their operations. In the summer of 1900 Curry and Annie teamed up with Lillie Davis, another of Fannie's girls, and Will Carver for a grand tour of the West. Lillie had grown up in Palestine in east Texas and found her way to employment at Fannie's to escape small-town life.

Carver, a handsome man, and Ben Kilpatrick—we will hear about him later—were both native Texans and probably introduced others of the gang to Fannie's sporting house. The two couples, Curry and Annie and Carver and Lillie, started their tour at the San Antonio Fair. From there they went to Denver and on to Idaho to see the Shoshone Falls.

The men left briefly to join other gang members and hold up a bank. The group returned to Denver, where Annie noticed that their luggage now included six or seven bags of gold, and both girls recalled that their luggage also contained much paper money. Kid Curry carried his favorite revolver in a valise, which someone stole while they were riding a train. He told Annie that it was hard to believe that anyone would be so cheap as to steal a man's gun!

In August the men said they had to go up the road a ways and would soon return. This time they held up a train in Tipton, Wyoming, and returned to Denver with more sacks of gold. Annie asked no questions about where the gold came from. Lillie, however, tearfully told Carver that she wanted to get married as she couldn't stand not being a respected woman. So they all returned to San Antonio, stopping in Fort Worth long enough for Carver and Lillie to be married.

Annie had moved another of Fannie's girls out of the picture to have Kid Curry for herself. After Curry escaped from jail in Tennessee, Annie followed him around the West until he committed suicide in June 1903, two days after being wounded in a Colorado train robbery. Annie then disappeared from history.

Carver kicked Lillie out before their first anniversary. Then he took up with Laura Bullion, who grew up on a farm in Tom Green County, a few miles from San Angelo. Laura's father had been killed while robbing a train, and she found her way to San Antonio and employment with Fannie.

When Carver was killed by Sheriff E. S. Briant in Sonora, Texas, on April 2, 1901, Laura took up with Ben Kilpatrick, another Texan. He was the tallest of the gang, usually called the Tall Texan. A handsome man like Carver, he was also illiterate.

He and Laura were arrested in St. Louis, where he got fifteen years in the federal prison and Laura got five. Laura didn't make history again. Kilpatrick was killed in March 1912, near Sanderson, Texas, while holding up a Southern Pacific train.

The most enduring relationship between a member of the Wild Bunch and one of Fannie Porter's girls was that of Etta Place and the Sundance Kid. He, like Carver and Kilpatrick, was described as handsome. Perhaps that is what it took to persuade the girls to take long leaves from the business.

Etta was a striking woman with lustrous auburn hair, soft brown eyes, and a quiet smile. She was recognized as the Sundance Kid's common-law wife, and though we don't know when the relationship began, it lasted the longest. She accompanied her lover and his partner, Butch Cassidy, to New York and to South America, where they introduced western-style outlawry to the Argentine pampas and the Bolivian jungles.

The final chapter in the American life of the Wild Bunch started in San Antonio after a bank robbery in Winnemucca, Nevada. The robbers on that job, Butch Cassidy, the Sundance Kid, and Carver, met at Fannie Porter's, as usual, to hide out. This time, however, they made a foolish mistake.

The gang usually wore felt hats at work, and, in a friendly scuffle with others of the gang, the hats were damaged. They saw some derby hats in a store window and decided to outfit themselves with what was then unusual headgear in the West. A few days later five of the gang—the three who held up the Winnemucca bank plus Kilpatrick and Kid Curry—were in Fort Worth.

On a whim, they stopped at a studio to have their photograph made, all wearing the new derby hats, along with suits, vests, and neckties. Until then, no one had looked for the gang in Texas, but Pinkerton detectives saw a copy of the photograph in the studio window in December 1900, and recognized some of the men. The investigation that followed put an end to the Wild Bunch.

A host of detectives came to Fort Worth, and the gang had its last rendezvous at Fannie Porter's. The men partied with Fannie's girls and cheered while Butch Cassidy rode a bicycle up and down the street, a scene replicated in the movie *Butch Cassidy and the Sundance Kid* starring Robert Redford and Paul Newman. Then the gang scattered.

The Sundance Kid and Butch Cassidy decided to move to South America. Accompanied by Etta Place, they reached New York City in February 1901. Posing as western cattlemen, they rented rooms as Mr. and Mrs. Harry Place and Jim Lowe (Cassidy). For the next three weeks the most wanted men in the country traveled about the city as tourists, buying expensive jewelry for Etta.

On February 20, after visiting a doctor in Buffalo, probably for treatment of venereal disease, Etta Place and the Sundance Kid sailed to Buenos Aires. Butch Cassidy returned to the West for one last robbery to finance their new lives in South America.

Cassidy was seen a few days later in Sonora, Texas, with Will Carver, but he had left for Arizona before Carver was killed. Then Cassidy picked up the Tall Texan, Kid Curry, and others to go to Montana and rob a Great Northern train between Malta and Wagner. Using dynamite to blow up a safe, they got between $40,000 and $80,000.

Cassidy soon headed for Argentina to join Etta and the Sundance Kid. Etta and her lover had deposited $12,000 in the bank when they first arrived. They stayed at a fashionable hotel, strolling about in formal clothes for two weeks, and then disappeared.

In April 1902, the Sundance Kid, signing as Harry E. Place, and Cassidy, signing as Santiago Ryan, filed a homestead petition to claim over fifteen thousand acres of land in Cholilo, in the Argentine province of Chubut. Cholilo was 250 miles south by boat from Buenos Aires and then fifteen days of hard riding to the west. Later that month the Sundance Kid and Etta returned to New York, where they went to Buffalo for more medical treatment.

In early August Etta and her lover returned to Buenos Aires. Cassidy had bought 1,300 sheep, 500 cattle, and 35 horses to stock their ranch. Etta and the Sundance Kid joined him there. By then Pinkerton detective Frank DiMaio was on their trail. He had the famous photo taken in Fort Worth and more photos taken in New York, which suggested that Etta Place was with them.

In March 1903, DiMaio showed the photos to a dentist in Buenos Aires who owned a ranch adjoining the homestead claim of the three Americans.

"I can't believe they're robbers," the dentist said. "They seem like such nice people."

Advised against trying to reach Cholilo in the rainy season, DiMaio passed out many wanted posters and returned to the United States.

Etta, her lover, and Cassidy ranched for three years, doubling their cattle and horse herds and improving the land.

But in March 1906, afraid of bounty hunters and bushwhackers, the three gave up their thriving ranch and returned to crime.

Etta held the horses as Cassidy and the Sundance Kid, joined by a young Texas outlaw named Dey who was on the dodge from warrants in the United States, held up the Banco de la Nación in Villa Mercedes, five hundred miles from Buenos Aires.

A month later, again with Etta as horse holder, Cassidy and the Sundance Kid got $20,000 from another Banco de la Nación robbery. They followed this with a train robbery in Bolivia, returning to Argentina to hide out.

Then the trio dropped out of sight, and we hear no more of Etta Place. Probably diseased, the Fannie Porter girl who stayed the longest with the Wild Bunch disappeared from history.

Butch Cassidy and the Sundance Kid were killed by a company of Bolivian cavalrymen in the small village of San Vincente in southwestern Bolivia in early 1909. They were wanted for stealing a mule from the tin mining company where they worked. They were buried in the Indian graveyard nearby.

Fannie Porter's brothel at the southwest corner of San Saba and Durango Streets (three blocks south of present Market Square) is no longer there. It stood for a long time, however, because of its location. The Ben Hur Social Club took over the house shortly after 1910. In 1914 Catholic Bishop J. W. Shaw purchased the home and used it as a residence for the Carmelite Sisters of the Divine Heart who had just arrived in San Antonio. There the sisters operated a home for poor, homeless children and a day nursery for children between ages one and six. When the sisters moved to new quarters eighty years later, the building became Father Flanagan's Girls and Boys Town of San Antonio.

The location is now part of a large parking area between the Holiday Inn and the San Antonio Expressway.

One report said that Fannie died in a streetcar accident in El Paso in 1912, but the death records there for 1912 do not list her. She certainly did leave her mark on Texas outlaw history.

Street Shoot-Out in Uvalde

When Uvalde County sheriff John Quincy Daugherty arrested
W. B. Owens the evening before, he knew that the rest of the
gang would soon be back. As he pushed his chair away from
the crudely constructed desk outside the second-floor jail in the
courthouse and rose slowly to his feet, he couldn't stop thinking of Sarah. She had come up the day before from their home,
which they had built near the protection of Fort Inge, two miles
away. That was March 17, 1865, the day his Irish forebearers in
Tennessee called St. Patrick's Day, and she had asked when he
was coming home to supper.

"I must stay here," he had said. "You know they'll be back
for him—probably early tomorrow." He had smiled at her
brown eyes and the worry lines in her still-attractive face. "Just
bring me a plate of something, Sarah."

Now, as he moved to the small outside platform at the end
of the room to check out the murmurings of a ruckus forming
in the street below, he remembered her later leaving with that
plate, scraped clean of potatoes, cabbage, and deer meat. She
had reached up and pressed her lips against his. When they
slowly separated, she whispered softly, "You take care now,
John. You've got a big family to see about."

He had grinned as he gently patted her lower abdomen.
"And getting bigger soon."

Now, after spending the night in his chair just outside the
jail door, he looked down to the dusty street. He wondered if
he would ever see his beloved Sarah again.

The leader of the gang slid his horse to a stop in front of the courthouse, waved a red flag, and demanded the release of the man in Daugherty's custody. As town militiamen moved quickly to the platform beside and behind him, Daugherty was surprised to recognize the Bates brothers, Baylus and Robert, riding with the gang. Their father, Elijah A. Bates, was one of the county's leading citizens.

Daugherty called out: "Now, it's best if you all just leave and let the law run its course."

The roar of guns answered his patient plea. Daugherty pitched forward and fell dead to the street below, a bloody hole in his forehead. He had commenced his duties as sheriff just five months before.

Still, this tale is not a typical account of a Texas shoot-out between bad men and the law. We don't know who named the gang the Owens Gang (sometimes called the Bad Owens Gang). No other incidents of criminal conduct can be found in the records except that some of the members were later indicted for another murder. We don't know what penalties resulted from this shoot-out because no one ever came to trial. Two of the gang later became prominent citizens, one of them a well-known lawman. The most interesting aspect was what the sheriff's wife had to endure—how this courageous woman handled her sudden widowhood was an example of the many strong women who had to carry on in the Old West.

Seventeen-year-old Thelia McKinney witnessed the shoot-out from a short distance away. Forty-eight years later her memory was still clear when she gave her account to the *San Antonio Express*. She said she saw Sheriff Daugherty fall from

Uvalde County Courthouse in 1865. *El Progreso Memorial Library, Archives and Museum, Uvalde, Texas*

the courthouse platform "pierced by bullets." Then a "pitched battle raged for thirty minutes."

Miss McKinney was placing a pan of milk in her kitchen safe when a bullet grazed her nose, knocking the pan from her hands. Her little brother and two of his friends suffered minor cuts from shattered glass, and the McKinney house was "riddled with bullets." Thelia told the newspaper that "some of the gang concealed themselves in the kitchen of the old Black residence just east of the courthouse. Here they opened fire on the courthouse and received a fierce volley in answer."

Miss McKinney added that she saw several occupants of the courthouse "leap from second story windows and retire hastily to safer quarters. When the battle was over, besides the dead sheriff only two men had been wounded. They were taken by stage to San Antonio where the bullets were extracted." She must have been referring to townspeople as all of the gang, including the one escaping from jail, got away. Sheriff Daugherty had been shot several times in the head and chest as he lay dead in the Uvalde street.

On May 3, 1865, the Uvalde County grand jury returned two true bills. One named W. S. B. Owens, W. P. Owens, W. J. Owens, G. W. Owens, Wiley Dodd, Baylus A. Bates, Robert Bates, Thomas Cooke, and James Cooke, charging the murder of John Q. Daugherty. The second named W. P. Owens, W. J. Owens, P. W. Owens, G. W. Owens, John Wilburn, Wiley Dodd, Baylus A. Bates, and George, the slave belonging to W. B. Owens, charging the "rescue" of W. B. Owens, a prisoner under the lawful custody of the sheriff.

Elijah A. Bates, father of two of the named defendants, was a member of the grand jury.

Some of the records in District Court Minute Book No. 1 of the 38th Judicial District of Texas are not dated; others are not in chronological order. The May 3 record showing the grand jury's true bills starts on page 230.

The filed indictments begin fourteen pages later. The murder charge listed P. W. Owens instead of G. W. Owens (probably the same person), and neither Cooke is mentioned. The unlawful escape charge also listed P. W. Owens instead of G. W., and it did not include the slave George.

A few days later a "W. S." Owens (not named exactly that way in the indictments) had surrendered himself into custody, and the murder defendants had apparently been arrested as their request for bail was granted. This appears on page 246 of the minute book.

The next entry of interest is dated April 30, 1866, almost a year later. It shows that the person appointed to act as sheriff by Andrew Jackson Hamilton, provisional governor of Texas during the reconstruction period, had declined to serve, and the judge of the district court had appointed William H. Pulliam instead.

So, after a year without a sheriff and probably without much law, Uvalde County, still reeling from Indian depredations and an unpopular Civil War—the county vote to secede was sixteen citizens for and seventy-six against—was poised to move forward in its law enforcement.

Not long after (undated but on page 310 of the minute book) the indictment for the unlawful "rescue" was dismissed on motion of the defendants. Wiley Dodd, one of the defendants, was dead by that time.

Also undated, page 330 of the minute book shows that the district attorney would not further prosecute murder defendant Robert Bates, and the indictment was dismissed as to him.

Again undated, page 345 shows that W. S. P. Owens and W. P. Owens were indicted for the murder of Joseph Robinson and that the indictment for the murder of John Daugherty was dismissed as to all the remaining defendants. My reading of the minute book (which has no index) stopped at the entries on June 6, 1871.

So none of the defendants charged with either the murder of John Daugherty or the unlawful escape of his prisoner was ever brought to trial.

Baylus Anderson Bates, eighteen at the time of the shootout, had run away from home at sixteen to join the Confederate Army. He was captured while fighting in a battle in Texas and held prisoner in New Orleans. Paroled at war's end, he married in September, 1871, in Frio County. Later he became a justice of the peace and commissioner in Zavala County. He joined the Texas Rangers and earned a reputation for maintaining law and order and "ridding the country of desperadoes."

Robert L. Bates, sixteen at the time of the shoot-out, married in 1866 and moved to Batesville, Texas, about 1875, where he ranched on land given him by his father.

The father of the Bates brothers, Elijah A. Bates, who was a member of the grand jury which indicted them, was a prominent Uvalde County merchant at the time of the shoot-out. He came to Texas from Alabama in 1852. He moved to Fort Inge in 1859. He kept a store there and later one in Uvalde. He founded Bates City in Zavala County, adjoining Uvalde County on the south. The city's name was later changed to Batesville.

It should not be surprising that the first defendant against whom the charges were dismissed was Robert L. Bates. We don't know how much of that decision was based on his youth at the time of the shoot-out and how much on the community esteem for his father.

W. S. B. Owens would become an original member of the Montel Guards, a militia company whose official title was Company G, Texas Volunteer Cavalry. The company was formed in 1881 for protection against Indians and "protection of life and property" in the frontier region north of Uvalde.

John and Sarah Pickett Daugherty had moved to Texas shortly after their marriage in 1851 in Ouachita County, Arkansas. He was twenty-three, two years older than his bride. They brought his mother with them to Texas, but Sarah would never again see her own mother.

John and Sarah stopped for a time in San Antonio, where son William was born on October 18, 1855. Soon after, the family settled on the Leona River, two miles south of present Uvalde. The small group of settlers there relied on the protection of Fort Inge, which had been established in 1849 to protect the San Antonio–El Paso Trail from Indians. About the time the Daughertys set up there in late 1855 or early 1856, the fort's military detachment of about one hundred men was moved to Fort Clark, forty miles west.

Renewed attacks by Indians on the now-unprotected settlers led the army to return to Fort Inge with a much smaller detachment in 1856. The fort consisted of ten or twelve buildings with a few *jacales*—hastily erected pole shelters daubed with mud. Since the original one-hundred-man detachment had been reduced to fewer than twenty with the reoccupation, very likely some of the settlers used the military buildings for their homes.

The Daughertys soon had a small herd of cattle, hogs, sheep, and goats. Sarah and her mother-in-law made and sold fruit pies to the soldiers. John was elected justice of the peace on November 17, 1856, and assessor–tax collector on May 7, 1857. Later that year, on August 31, 1857, Sarah gave birth to their second son, James.

In 1859, one of the worst years for Indian depredations in that part of Texas, John Daugherty was elected deputy sheriff. He also served as leader of a local militia to assist the army in its fight against the Indians. In October of that year, he led twenty-eight militiamen assisting thirteen cavalrymen under the command of Lt. William Babcock Hazen from Fort Inge.

The combined force attacked Comanches who had killed two settlers. After two days of a running battle along twenty miles of the Frio and Sabinal Rivers, at least a half dozen Indians had been killed. One of them was carrying the scalp of one of the settlers who had been killed and another had the scalps of three young children. At least three of Daugherty's militiamen were wounded in the battle.

The extra duties of fighting Indians apparently made it impossible to serve as assessor–tax collector in addition to deputy sheriff. Daugherty's friend, DeWitt Clinton Rain, became assessor–tax collector in October, 1859, to replace Daugherty. Rain, a member of William R. Henry's company of Rangers, also fought Indians in Frio and Sabinal canyons.

Although Uvalde County citizens (and those in many other counties) had voted against secession, Texas still seceded from the United States in March 1861. Daugherty enlisted in the Texas Cavalry in Uvalde and was later transferred as an officer into another cavalry regiment in Clarksville in northeast Texas. By then he and Sarah had a third son, Thomas Paine, born April 11, 1860, at Fort Inge. A daughter, Louisa Jane, would be born March 12, 1862, also at Fort Inge.

Daugherty served in action against Union forces in Arkansas and Louisiana. He became disgusted with the war, writing his family that "the poor man is forced into the army, and the rich man is at home speculating, making a fortune off the widows and orphans of deceased soldiers."

When Texas seceded in 1861, the federal troops were removed from Fort Inge and, again, Indians attacked. Confederate troops occupied the fort from time to time, but life for Sarah and other settlers must have been chancy at best. Very likely the small community felt relief when the veterans of the Civil War—whether Union or Confederate—returned to take up their lives again. Lt. Hazen who, with Daugherty, had led the small force against Comanches in 1859 would be a Union general by the end of the war.

On August 1, 1864, while he was still serving in the Confederate Army in northeast Texas, Daugherty was elected sheriff of Uvalde County. He signed his oath of office in Tyler (Smith County) on August 22. When he learned that Sarah's mother had died the month before, he traveled home from the war by way of McKinney, near Dallas. There he picked up Sarah's two sisters, Martha and Marinda, now orphans, and carried them in an oxcart to Uvalde, where they were welcomed into the Daugherty household.

With a slow ox setting the pace, Daugherty and his sisters-in-law, Marinda, sixteen, and Martha, a year or two older, did not reach Uvalde until early October. He posted his performance bond on October 3 and assumed his duties as sheriff.

As Sarah felt her fifth baby quicken in her body that winter of 1864–65, her spirits must have improved as well. William, just turning ten, James, seven, Thomas Paine, four, and Louisa Jane, two, would have filled her primitive home with sounds of joy. Her sisters would have grown so much since she had last seen them, thirteen years before. Then they were like her own children; now they would talk about learning new housekeeping skills and, in hushed voices, about the young men in the community. It was probably the most pleasant time Sarah would know before her world crashed around her on that dreadful day in March.

We have no letters from Sarah telling how she survived the rest of 1865; she was probably too busy to write. We don't

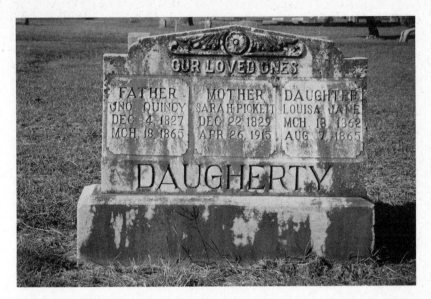

Daugherty family tombstone. *Author's photo collection*

know if she—perhaps unconsciously—urged her sisters into matrimony. Perhaps the girls took action on their own, or perhaps nature just took its course. Marinda married DeWitt Clinton Rain, John's good friend who had succeeded him as county assessor–tax collector, on August 3.

Four days later, on August 7, three-year-old Louisa Jane died.

Less than a month later, Martha married John S. Watts on September 2.

Sarah must have thought she was living in an emotional tornado with the murder of her husband, the death of her daughter, and the marriages of her two sisters. One more event would bring the seven-month travail to an end. John Quincy Daugherty, Junior, was born on October 29, 1865.

Two of the Daugherty sons, James and John Jr., became well drillers. In 1900 they built a home for their mother in

141

Alpine in West Texas. Later they and their mother moved to Olney in Young County, where Sarah died on April 26, 1915, aged eighty-four. She was buried in the Uvalde cemetery in the same plot where her husband and their daughter had been interred so much earlier.

Marinda and her husband, DeWitt Clinton Rain, my wife's great grandparents, eventually moved to Marshall in northeast Texas, where they are buried in the Crossroads Cemetery.

John Quincy Daugherty's name has been engraved on the Texas Peace Officers Memorial in Austin and on the National Law Enforcement Officers Memorial in Washington D.C.

Sarah Daugherty's name, along with her husband's and daughter's, has been engraved on the family tombstone in the Uvalde Cemetery. This Texas woman who had to rely on a reduced complement of soldiers at a federal fort for protection against Indians when her husband and others left to fight in a civil war, had only her own courage and character to carry her through seven difficult months of pregnancy after her husband's murder. Who knows how many names on early Texas tombstones identify other women whose stories can never be told?

A Good Man Gone Bad

In May 1894, Bill Dalton and Jim Wallace camped on the Sabine River to plan their robbery of the First National Bank in nearby Longview, Texas. A few months earlier, Wallace had married the daughter of a Longview farmer, but he deserted her and returned to Indian Territory (present Oklahoma) where his brother Houston farmed near Ardmore. There he found Dalton hiding out after serving as second-in-command of Bill Doolin's band of robbers, which had been holding up banks and trains in Indian Territory.

"That Longview bank's jist waitin' to be robbed," Wallace had told him.

"I'm interested. Tell me about it."

Dalton realized, as soon as Wallace took him to Longview, that more than two men would be required. They enlisted the Knight brothers, Asa and Jim, who worked at the Brown and Flewellen sawmill seven miles north of town, and then finalized their plans.

Late on the rainy afternoon of May 23, the four men rode into Longview from the west. A local doctor recognized Jim Knight and called out to remind him of an overdue fee.

"That's whar I'm goin' now, Doc," Knight answered. "To the bank fer some money."

The four outlaws swung down from their horses in front of the bank on Tyler Avenue. Wallace and Asa Knight led the horses north up Fredonia Street to an alley behind the bank. Dalton and Jim Knight entered the bank through the front door and asked for the president, Joe Clemmons, who was conducting business with a customer. When Clemmons turned to him, Dalton handed him this note, penciled on the back of a poster:

MAY 23, 1894
TO CASHIER, FIRST NAT. BANK, LONGVIEW:
THIS WILL INTRODUCE YOU TO CHAS. SPECKLEMEYER, WHO
WANTS SOME MONEY AND WILL HAVE IT.
B AND F.

Some speculate that "B and F" meant Bill and Friends, and it appeared that Dalton had used the name Charles Specklemeyer before in Indian Territory.

At first Clemmons thought the note was a request for a charitable contribution, and he turned to get the money. Then his brother, cashier Tom Clemmons, saw Dalton draw a revolver as Jim Knight approached the vault with a burlap bag. The cashier jumped Dalton and grabbed at his revolver.

Dalton pulled the trigger, but the hammer fell on the web of flesh between Clemmons's thumb and forefinger.

By then merchant John Welborne had entered the bank, saw the scuffle, and ran back outside, followed by bank employee Josh Cooke. "They're robbing the bank," both men shouted.

Some citizens ran for cover but others ran for the bank. The latter included George Buckingham, bartender at Jerry Munden's saloon, three doors away. Buckingham grabbed a pistol and ran out into the street. Wallace saw him from the alley where he and Asa Knight held the horses.

Wallace had stuffed three hundred rounds of ammunition into his saddlebags, and he was anxious to start shooting. He opened fire with his Winchester rifle, and the brave bartender fell, the first to die on that terrible day.

When Wallace aimed again at Buckingham, Mrs. McCulloch who ran a boardinghouse across the street screamed, "Don't shoot him anymore. You've already killed him."

Wallace kept firing. His next victim was the city marshal, Matt Muckleroy, who had all the luck that escaped Buckingham. Wallace's bullet hit a silver dollar in Muckleroy's shirt pocket and ricocheted downward into the marshal's abdomen. The lawman would recover.

Charles S. Learned, a local mill owner, was next to fall in Wallace's rampage. He was shot through the leg. Doctors would amputate, but Learned died two days later.

Wallace then dropped J. Walter McQueen who eventually recovered from his wound. Wallace followed this with a shot at a "slightly retarded man" who was sitting on a box, minding his own business, in front of the saloon. The bullet grazed the man's head and entered the saloon where it ripped off part of T. C. Summers's finger as he stood at the bar nursing a drink.

By this time, attorney Charles Lacy had found a rifle, and he ran into a feed store adjacent to the bank. He fired at Wallace's back from an alley window, and Wallace fell dead in his tracks.

Asa Knight, Wallace's partner in the alley, fired two shots at Lacy's window, but both went wild. Between 250 and 300 rounds of ammunition had been spent in a span of three minutes, but the battle had ended.

Dalton and Jim Knight, forcing the Clemmons brothers ahead of them, reached the alley through the bank's rear door. When Dalton saw Wallace dead or dying, he only said, "poor Jim," and the three surviving outlaws mounted their horses and

Jim Wallace's rifle and Marshal Muckleroy's pistol (top) in the Historic
Museum, Longview. *Author's photo collection*

headed west on Tyler Avenue. They forced their two hostages to mount Wallace's horse and ride double. About a mile out of town they released the bank officers and then rode on at a faster speed.

Even then, Dalton's penchant for unusual notes reappeared. When the escaping robbers came upon a lone traveler, Dalton stopped long enough to motion toward his pursuers and hand the man two Winchester cartridges with this note:

> YOU'LL GET PLENTY OF THESE IF YOU FOLLOW TOO CLOSE.
> CHARLES SPECKLEMEYER

By this time Gregg County Sheriff Jack Howard had led a posse into the thick pine forest surrounding Longview, but they turned back empty-handed. Some even claimed that Howard had said, "Let's go back, boys. Maybe we're getting too close."

In the meantime angry Longview citizens dragged Wallace's body to a telegraph pole close to the Texas and Pacific Railway depot. They put a noose around the corpse's neck, hoisted it fifteen feet in the air, called a photographer, and posed for pictures.

Wallace's hatband contained a label from W. O. Dunstan's Big Cash Store in Ardmore of the Chickasaw Nation in Indian Territory, and the authorities there were notified.

On Monday, June 4, two men showed up at Duncan, fifty miles northwest of Ardmore. They bought a new wagon with ten- and twenty-dollar bills. The bills looked new. Deputy marshals at Ardmore telegraphed the bill numbers to Longview and learned that they were taken in the robbery.

Three days later, farmer Houston Wallace (Jim Wallace's brother) accompanied by his wife and "a pretty blonde about twenty-seven" drove into Ardmore in a wagon. They paid cash for ammunition and a large supply of groceries. Houston was considered a "worthless fellow who never had a dime," and Deputy Marshal Selden T. Lindsey was immediately called. He found Wallace at the express office picking up nine quarts of whiskey. Wallace said the whiskey was for friends staying at his home, midway between Ardmore and Duncan.

It was illegal to bring whiskey into Indian Territory, so Lindsey ordered Wallace and the two women held for questioning. Then he organized a posse of six deputy marshals and two Indian policemen, and they traveled all night to reach the Wallace farm at eight o'clock the next morning.

While the posse took positions surrounding the house, a man stepped outside to look around. Seeing the officers, he leaped back inside, grabbed a revolver, jumped back out a window, and ran for a small ravine in Russell Pretty Branch Creek. He reportedly kept two horses saddled there for an emergency, but he never reached the ravine.

Deputy Marshal Caleb (Loss) Hart, less than forty yards away, shouted "Halt!" The man half turned and had his revolver raised to fire when Hart's .44 rifle bullet tore into his body.

Hart raced to the fallen man's side, grabbed his revolver, and shouted, "Who are you? Where are you from?" The man smiled as though happy that he had not been recognized and died without a word.

The officers found six small, frightened children inside the house, along with many rolls of crisp bank bills. Two of the children admitted that their name was Dalton.

The marshals found a wagon, loaded the body into it, and started for Ardmore, about twenty-five miles away. As they neared the town, they met another wagon containing Houston Wallace's wife and the "pretty blonde." They had just been released from the investigation that started the day before.

"Mrs. Dalton," Deputy Marshal Lindsey said, "we have your husband and we found considerable money . . ."

"I'm not Mrs. Dalton and you don't have Bill."

But when she looked at the body, she broke down and admitted that it was her husband.

We have to go back a few years to a train robbery in California to get perspective on the events that lead to Bill Dalton's death in Indian Territory.

Like their cousins, the Youngers, the Dalton brothers were steeped in the violence, hatred, and crime that marked the Middle Border states for years after the Civil War. Their mother, Adaline Younger Dalton, married at fifteen, less than half the age of her husband, Lewis, who loved whiskey, gambling, and racing horses. She had fifteen children, twelve of them surviving infancy. Of those, three were daughters and one a sickly boy who died at fourteen. The remaining eight brothers can be divided into two groups with Bill somewhere in between.

Bob and Emmett, both younger than Bill, and Grat, two years older, started out as deputy marshals in Indian Territory, but soon left that career for stealing horses and other forms of outlawry. Littleton, Cole, Frank, and Ben, all older than Bill, were law-abiding. They spent much of their adult lives in California. Bill started out like his older, saner brothers, but he would change.

Bill Dalton moved to California to stay in 1884, when he was twenty-one. Before that he had visited his father from time to time as Lewis Dalton raced his string of not-very-fast horses at California tracks. Now a grown man, Bill worked for Cyrus Bliven, a wealthy wheat grower in Livingston, Merced County. After marrying Bliven's oldest daughter, Jane, Bill Dalton operated a ranch in partnership with Jane's brother, Clark Bliven, in the northeast corner of San Luis Obispo County, near Cholame. Bill and Jane would eventually have two children, Charles (Chub) and Gracie.

During the years 1888 and 1889, Grat, Bob, and Emmett visited Bill and Littleton Dalton from time to time. Littleton was operating a saloon during some of that time, and he soon learned that his brothers were hiding from Indian Territory officials who wanted them for stealing horses. He warned his brothers that "it was only the beginning for them and that they would end up by stretching rope or by stopping a Winchester bullet apiece."

About a week after Littleton gave his brothers the warning, Bill Dalton came over from his ranch to talk about their brothers. "We talked the biggest part of two days," Littleton said. "Bill told me what the boys had been telling him. The story that they told me was the same. Bill was just as worried as I was."

Littleton told Bill that they should tell their brothers that they would turn them in immediately to local officers if they did anything to break the law. But Bill was not so sure.

"Bill, there is no use going any farther with them," Littleton said. "In a short time they'll kill somebody, and then they'll get the rope."

Cole and Ben had also been giving the same advice to their brothers. But Bill was adamant. "You fellows are all wrong," he said. "As long as I don't break with the boys, I can do something with them to change their minds."

Littleton thought that was the worst mistake Bill ever made. "He had never been in any trouble," Littleton said. "He was a well-respected farmer and politician. He was then Democratic Central Committee chairman in Merced County and also a political committeeman near Estrella."

Littleton summed it up: "Bill never broke with the boys, but they sure broke him. When Bob and Emmett and Grat finally finished with him he was a bum; his stock and farming equipment were gone and he was broke; and he was finally killed running an outlaw band of his own."

Bill and Cole tried for a month to get their outlaw brothers to settle down in honest employment. The three men would work a few days at a time driving mule teams for the Dalton-Bliven Ranch; then they would play poker and get into fistfights in Paso Robles, San Luis Obispo, or San Miguel. Bill tried to get them on at a Miller & Lux ranch near Firebaugh, where he knew the superintendent. He even drove to neighbors to borrow saddles and riding equipment so the brothers could work. When they left, they took two of Bill's plow horses for part of their wages, which Bill hadn't money enough to pay.

Shortly after they left, Bill discovered that his brothers had cut a trapdoor in a closet ceiling of his house, and he feared that they were planning on hiding there if necessary.

On the evening of February 6, 1891, Southern Pacific's Atlantic Express from San Francisco to Los Angeles made a very brief stop in the mountain village of Alila (now Earlimont), about sixty miles east of Cholame. Bob and Emmett Dalton, weapons drawn, boarded the train during the stop. Although the express car carried eleven sacks of silver worth $9,700, the car was locked from the inside by express messenger C. C. Haswell, and Bob and Emmett's first attempt at train robbery failed. However, fireman George W. Radliff was mortally wounded (dying the next day) by Haswell, shooting out from the window of his locked car. Bob and Emmett mounted their horses, which they had tied nearby, and rode west as fast as the plow horses could go.

Bob and Emmett reached Cholame and made contact with Bill. He knew that they were in some trouble and didn't want them in his house. They hid out in the mountains for a couple of weeks, and Bill put food and supplies out for them. Eventually he learned about the attempted train robbery and feared that his brothers had been involved.

Eugene W. Kay, Tulare County sheriff, and a deputy followed the tracks of two unshod horses and two booted men west from the site of the attempted robbery. It took several days to trail them to Bill Dalton's home. Jane Dalton and her two little children were there. She invited the officers to stay for supper. During the meal, Bill arrived and invited the officers to spend the night, which they did.

Sheriff Kay got up early and went to the barn to feed and water his and his deputy's horses the next morning. On the trail west from Alila he had found a piece of wood that had broken off recently from a stirrup. While caring for the horses, he found a hidden saddle. It had a broken place in the stirrup that exactly matched the piece of wood. Kay woke his deputy, and they slipped out of the house and rode away to continue their investigation.

By this time Bill Dalton knew that Bob and Emmett had tried to rob a train. Thankfully Grat was not involved, although he may have known about the attempt. Bill would not have to worry about Grat, but he decided to help Bob and Emmett get out of California. They hadn't gotten anything from the foiled attempt but experience; perhaps they'd learn from that and reform. He was tired of trying to teach his wayward brothers anything. Stealing horses in Indian Territory was bad enough; now they had tried to rob a train in California! If they didn't learn from that, maybe they'd try bank robbery!

Bill was glad to learn that Littleton, who was working south of Fresno and had always lived a straight-arrow life, had also decided to help Bob and Emmett get away. Their resolve to help their brothers increased when they learned that Emmett had mistakenly thought that he had fired the shot that killed fireman Radliff. Radliff had died the day after the attempted robbery. For both Bill and Littleton, their help for their brothers was a onetime deal. The brothers either had to shape up or they were through with them.

Using horses obtained by Littleton, Bill rode with his brothers down the west side of the San Joaquin Valley and turned east to cross the Tehachapi Mountains and enter the Mohave Desert. Bill left them at Bealville, and he traveled on ahead by train. He wanted to establish a hideout somewhere near the railroad so his brothers could travel on ahead by train as soon as it was safe. They made this change at Ludlow, Bob and Emmett going ahead to Indian Territory and Bill returning to Paso Robles.

Sheriff Kay arrested Bill Dalton for the Alila train robbery within fifteen minutes of his stepping off the train at Paso Robles. The three bondsmen who posted bail for him were an ex-county supervisor, the father of a deputy sheriff, and one of the county's leading merchants.

Sheriff Kay spent the next three months on a six thousand mile trail through seven states and parts of Mexico trying to find Bob and Emmett Dalton without success. But Bill Dalton, who had had nothing to do with the train robbery, would not stand trial alone. His brother Grat was also indicted.

Grat Dalton certainly knew about the plans to rob a southbound Southern Pacific train near Alila. He and his brothers had finalized their plans in Delano, where he expected to buy a horse. But when Grat got through playing poker, he didn't have enough money for a horse, so he had ridden a freight train north, apparently expecting to meet his brothers after the robbery. His northbound freight had to wait on a siding at Alila for a southbound express to clear the track before it could move on. Later Grat would learn that the train his was waiting on was the train his brothers tried to rob. It would have been impossible for Grat to be one of the robbers.

While he waited for the trial, Bill Dalton pondered about the justice of charging two innocent men for a crime just because the authorities could not find the brothers who had committed the crime.

Grat's trial began in Visalia in June, 1891. His lawyer was John W. Breckenridge, whose father had been vice president of the United States and who was reportedly the best criminal defense lawyer in California. Bill had hired Breckenridge to represent both Grat and himself at their trials, but Bill's trial wasn't to be until October. Not until after his own trial would Bill learn that his lawyer was also a consultant for the Southern Pacific Railroad.

After the longest and most expensive trial in Tulare County history, the jury returned a verdict of guilty against

Grat. Now Bill pondered more about justice, as he waited for his own trial.

On the night of September 20, Grat and two other inmates escaped from the Tulare County jail with the help of files and digging tools smuggled in by outsiders. Another version of the escape (described by more than one writer) illustrates how the exploits of the Daltons were often exaggerated in California.

In this more colorful version, Grat Dalton was being transferred by train to prison to serve his twenty-year sentence. As the train ran next to the swift-running San Joaquin River, Grat, while handcuffed to two armed deputies and with his feet tied together, jumped up and dove headfirst out a train window into the river below. The screaming passengers saw him plunge into the river and disappear. All the deputies found when the train stopped were fresh hoofprints from two horses. Listeners to the tale would have no trouble guessing who held the waiting horses and helped his brother escape.

After the real Grat and two other inmates dug their way out of the real jail, one inmate was captured, but Grat made his way to Indian Territory and he would never serve a day of his prison sentence.

Bill Dalton's trial started on October 5, and the jury returned a not guilty verdict on October 10 after fifteen minutes of deliberation. Bill probably pondered about justice even more when he wondered why he and his brother had to defend themselves in jury trials, and why Grat's jury had found him guilty.

Despondent at the way he and his brothers had been treated by the law in California and unsure what the brothers would do after they reached Indian Territory, Bill Dalton returned to his mother's home in Kingfisher (his father had died in 1890).

But first he sold his ranch at Cholame and moved Jane and the children to her parents' home near Livingston. On his ride back to Kingfisher, Bill's tortured mind struggled with the choice of following his brothers into crime or trying again to talk them out of it. One way would be best for them and their mother, but his own mental state and his loss of faith in the justice of California courts pointed a different way

Bill reached his mother's cabin in late January 1892, and he learned that Bob and Emmett had gathered a few confederates and were robbing trains and hiding out in the Cheyenne and Arapaho country west of Kingfisher.

Grat arrived a few days later. He had lost forty pounds and looked terrible. His horse looked worse and died a few days later. Bill gave up trying to preach reform, but he was still unwilling to become an active member of the Dalton Gang, then led by Bob. Bill became an "outside spy" and an occasional "advisor."

The Dalton Gang was not taking any advice from Bill when they decided to hold up two banks at the same time in Coffeyville, Kansas, a place where the Dalton brothers were well known. The attempted robbery on October 5, 1892, was Bob's idea and planned by him. He, Grat, and their two confederates were killed that day, and Emmett would be sentenced to life in prison.

When he heard about his brothers' idiotic attempt, Bill Dalton became convinced that Coffeyville citizens had "looted" his brothers in the way they attacked them, stole from their clothing after they were killed, and exhibited their dead bodies. He swore to get even with society and joined Bill Doolin's band of robbers as second-in-command.

After more train and bank robberies, the Doolin Gang established headquarters in Ingalls, a small town fifty miles northeast of Kingfisher. On September 1, 1893, thirty deputy US marshals attacked the seven Doolin Gang members in the town. When the shooting stopped, three deputies and a town youth lay dead, and three citizens and an innocent bystander, plus two of the Doolin Gang, were wounded. Bill Dalton escaped injury, but three of his bullets were in the body of one of the deputies.

Bill decided that Indian Territory was too hot for him. When Jim Wallace suggested the robbery of the Texas bank, he was ready to go.

After Jane Dalton admitted that the body in the marshal's wagon was Bill, she followed the wagon back to Ardmore. There she said that Bill had sold their California home two years before to return to Oklahoma Territory. She had no thought that he was not living an honest life, but she followed him in September 1893, and he had failed to meet her on her arrival. When he called on her the following night, she wondered why he was so heavily armed.

"We came to the Wallace place six weeks ago," Jane Dalton continued. "He engaged board for myself and the children, saying he was going to Texas. I heard nothing more of him until . . ."

Jane Dalton took her husband's body back to California and buried it at Livingston, next to her parents' home.

Clarence B. Douglas, correspondent for the *Daily Oklahoman,* closed his report about the Longview, Texas, robbery:

It has often been said that when Bill Dalton died he
would go to the shadowy land accompanied by a number
of persons and that any man who faced him in the last
great duel of his life would bear him company. But
he was killed like some pitiable chicken thief and the
glamour of romance and daring thrown around his life
by his brave and lawless deeds before his death prove
once more that law and justice are supreme and must in
the end be triumphant.

Bibliography

Family Man

El Paso Times, April 17 and April 24, 1895.

Hardin, John Wesley. *Life of John Wesley Hardin as Written by Himself.* Norman: University of Oklahoma Press, 1961.

Jennings, N. A. *A Texas Ranger.* New York: Charles Scribner's Sons, 1899.

John Wesley Hardin Collection, Southwestern Writers Collection, Texas State University, San Marcos, Box 174, Folders 1, 2, and 4.

Family Troubles

Holden, Frances M. *Lambshead Before Interwoven.* College Station: Texas A & M University Press, 1982.

Hunter, J. Marvin. *The Story of Lottie Deno.* Bandera: The 4 Hunters, 1959.

Metz, Leon C. *John Selman: Texas Gunfighter.* New York: Random House, 1966.

Rister, Carl C. *Fort Griffin on the Texas Frontier.* Norman: University of Oklahoma Press, 1956.

Rye, Edgar. *The Quirt and the Spur.* Austin: Steck-Vaughn Company, 1967.

Sonnichsen, C. L. *I'll Die Before I'll Run*. New York: The Devin-Adair Company, 1962.

Death Dances on the Border

Collinson, Frank. *Life in the Saddle*. Norman: University of Oklahoma Press, 1963.
———. "Three Texas Triggermen." *Ranch Romances*, July 1936.
Metz, Leon C. *John Selman: Texas Gunfighter*. New York: Random House, 1966.
———. Personal papers. Box 20, Folders 23, 60. Special Collections, University of Texas, El Paso.

Born to Hang

Shirley, Glenn. *Shotgun for Hire*. Norman: University of Oklahoma Press, 1970.
Sonnichsen, C. L. *Ten Texas Feuds*. Albuquerque: University of New Mexico Press, 1957.
———. *Tularosa*. New York: The Devin-Adair Company, 1961.

A Foolish Boast

Capps, Benjamin. *The Warren Wagon Train Raid*. New York: Dial Press, 1974.
"Eureka." *Army and Navy Journal* 8, no. 48 (July 15, 1871).

Hamilton, Allen Lee. "The Warren Wagontrain Raid."
Arizona and the West, 28 (Autumn 1986).

Mayhall, Mildred P. *The Kiowas*. Norman: University of
Oklahoma Press, 1962.

Nye, W. S. *Carbine and Lance: The Story of Old Fort Sill*.
Norman: University of Oklahoma Press, 1943.

Wilbarger, J. W. *Indian Depredations in Texas*. Austin:
Hutchings Printing House, 1889.

Misdirected Vengeance from "Those Californians"

Haley, J. Evetts. "L'Archévèque, the Outlaw." *The Shamrock
Magazine*, Fall 1958.

McCarty, John L. *Maverick Town: The Story of Old Tascosa*.
Norman: University of Oklahoma Press, 1946.

Parkman, Francis. *La Salle and the Discovery of the Great
West*. Boston: Little, Brown, and Co., 1880.

Turner, George. "A Killer's Legacy of Terror." *Amarillo
Sunday News Globe*, September 25, 1966.

He Was a Man before He Was Done Being a Boy

Bartholomew, Ed. *Wild Bill Longley: A Texas Hard Case*.
Giddings, Texas: privately published by Woodrow
Wilson, 1953. Reprint, 1969.

Cunningham, Eugene. *Triggernometry: A Gallery of
Gunfighters*. Caldwell, ID: The Caxton Printers, 1952.

Killen, Mrs. James C., ed. *History of Lee County, Texas*.
Quanah, TX: Nortex Press, 1974.

State of Texas v. William P. Longley, Case No. 100, Criminal
 Minutes Book A, District Court for Lee County, Texas,
 1877, 1878.

A Woman Who Saw Much of Life

Austin Daily Statesman, April 9 and April 17, 1874.
Marriage record of James C. Reed and Myra Belle Shirley,
 recorded November 11, 1866, in Volume 3, Page 49,
 Marriage Records of Collin County, Texas.
Rascoe, Burton. *Belle Starr, the Bandit Queen*. New York:
 Random House, 1941.
Shackleford, William Yancey. *Belle Starr, the Bandit Queen*.
 Girard, Kansas: Haldeman-Julius, 1943.
Shirley, Glenn. *Belle Starr and Her Times*. Norman:
 University of Oklahoma Press, 1982.
West Texas Free Press, April 11, 18, and 25; May 2; August
 15; and September 5, 1874.

Two Cities Give Up the Wild West

Cunningham, Eugene. *Triggernometry: A Gallery of
 Gunfighters*. Caldwell, ID: The Caxton Printers, 1952.
Fisher, O. C. *King Fisher: His Life and Times*. Norman:
 University of Oklahoma Press, 1966.
San Antonio Daily Express, March 12 and 13, 1884.
Walton, W. M. *Life and Adventures of Ben Thompson*. Austin:
 self-published, 1884.

Two Friends in the Hoo Doo War

Austin Daily Statesman, October 17, 1875, November 9, 1876.

Burrows, Jack. *Johnny Ringo: The Gunfighter Who Never Was.* Tucson: University of Arizona Press, 1987.

Gillett, James B. *Six Years with the Texas Rangers.* New Haven: Yale University Press, 1925.

Houston Daily Telegraph, March 3, 1875.

Johnson, David. *The Mason County "Hoo Doo" War.* Denton: University of North Texas Press, 2006.

San Antonio Herald, August 18, 1874, September 14, 1875.

Border Bandits

Dobie, J. Frank. *A Vaquero of the Brush Country.* London: Hammond, Hammond, & Co., 1949.

Paredes, Américo. *With His Pistol in His Hand: A Border Ballad and Its Hero.* Austin: University of Texas Press, 1958.

Stuart, Ben C. "The Rio Grande Raiders." *The Texas Magazine,* March 1910, 46–50.

Thompson, Jerry D. *Juan Cortina and the Texas–Mexico Frontier.* El Paso: Texas Western Press, 1994.

US Congress. House. *Texas Border Troubles.* 45th Cong., 1st sess., serial 1820. H. Misc. Doc. 64.

———. *Troubles on the Texas Frontier.* 36th Cong., 1st sess., serial 1056. H. Exec. Doc. 81.

Rest and Recuperation in Texas

Appler, Jules A. General Directory of the City of San Antonio, 1897–98.

Bowser, David. *West of the Creek*. San Antonio: Maverick Publishing Company, 2003.

Bowser, David C. "Fannie Porter's House." *Journal of the Western Outlaw—Lawmen History Association*, Summer 1995.

DiMaio, Frank. "Recollections of Trailing Butch Cassidy, the Sundance Kid and Etta Place in South America, New York City, and New York State." The James D. Horan Civil War and Western Americana Collection.

Selcer, Richard. *Hell's Half Acre*. Fort Worth: Texas Christian University Press, 1991.

Street Shoot-Out in Uvalde

Clippings folder, El Progreso Memorial Library. Uvalde, Texas.

District Court Minute Book Number 1, 38th Judicial District of Texas, Uvalde, Texas.

San Antonio Express, September 28, 1913.

Sowell, A. J. *Early Settlers and Indian Fighters of Southwest Texas*. New York: Argosy-Antiquarian Ltd., 1964.

A Good Man Gone Bad

Daily Ardmoreite, June 9, 1894.

Daily Oklahoman, June 14, 1894.

Latta, Frank F. *Dalton Gang Days*. Santa Cruz: Bear State Books, 1976.

O'Neal, Bill. "Bill Dalton's Last Raid." *Real West*, June 1983.

Shirley, Glenn. *Six-Gun and Silver Star*. Albuquerque: University of New Mexico Press, 1955.

The Dallas Morning News, May 25, 1894.

Index

Rio Grande, xxi, 90, 110, 112, 113, 119
Rio Grande City, Texas, 113
Rio Grande Valley, 113
Ripley County, 109
Ripley, Robert, xix, 65
Robertson County, 33
Robinson, Joseph, 136
Robledo, Martín, 118
Rocky Ford, Colorado, 15
Rodríguez, Ramón, 118, 119
Rogers, Annie, 123, 125, 126
Romula Granadino. *See* Selman, Romula
Roosevelt, Theodore, 41
Russell Pretty Branch Creek, 148
Ryan, Santiago. *See* Cassidy, Butch
Rye, Edgar, 24, 25

S

Sabinal River, 139
Sabine River, 143
Salt Creek Prairie, 46
San Angelo, Texas, 126
San Antonio Daily Express, 97
San Antonio-El Paso Trail, 138
San Antonio Express, 133
San Antonio Expressway, 131
San Antonio Fair, 125
San Antonio Herald, 102
San Antonio National Bank, 84
San Antonio River, 119
San Antonio, Texas, xx, xxi, xxiii, 80, 84, 89, 123, 126, 127, 130, 135
San Antonio to Austin stage, 84
Sanderson, Texas, 127
Sandoval, Martín, 118
San Francisco, 152
San Joaquin River, 155
San Joaquin Valley, 153
San Jose, California, 104
San Luis Obispo, California, 151
San Luis Obispo County, 150
San Marcos River, 84
San Marcos, Texas, 84
San Miguel, California, 151
Santa Anna Mountains, 70
Santa Fe Trail, 70
San Vincente, Bolivia, 130
Sapello, New Mexico Territory, 57
Satank, 45, 46, 47, 48
Satanta (White Bear), xviii, 45

Sawyer, Lon, xix, 70, 71, 72
Scarborough, George, xvii, 26, 29, 30, 31, 32
Schnabel, Henry, 118, 119, 121
Schnabel ranch, 118
Scyene, Texas, 79, 82, 86
Second Texas Cavalry, 90, 91
Selman, John, xvi, 13, 17, 19, 21, 22, 23, 24, 25, 26
Selman, John, Junior, 12, 29, 31, 32
Selman, Nicanora, xvii, 27, 28
Selman, Romula, 28
Selman, Tom, 27
Shackelford County, xvi, xvii, 14, 15, 17, 21, 27
Shaw, J. W., 130
Sherman, William T., 46, 47, 48, 49
Shield's Boarding House, 14, 24
Shirley, Bud, 77, 79
Shirley, Cravens, 80
Shirley, Edwin, 80
Shirley, John, 79, 82
Shirley, John Allison. *See* Shirley, Bud
Shirley, Myra Belle. *See* Starr, Belle
Shoshone Falls, 126
Silver City, New Mexico Territory, 58, 62
Simms, Billy, 91, 95, 96
Slack, R. A., 25
Smith County, 140
Sonora, Texas, 126, 128
South America, xxiii, 127, 128
Soward, Charles, 49, 51, 52, 53, 54
Spaniard, Jack, 87
Specklemeyer, Charles. *See* Dalton, Bill
Starr, Belle, xx, 74, 77
Starr, Sam, 87
St. Joseph, 69
St. Louis, 127
St. Patrick's Day, 132
St. Paul, Minnesota, 84
Summers, T. C., 145
Sundance Kid, xxiii, 123, 127, 128, 129, 130, 131
Sutton, Bill, 7
Sutton-Taylor feud, 7, 66

T

Tall Texan, the. *See* Kilpatrick, Ben
Tamaulipas, Mexico, xxii
Tascosa, Texas, 61, 64
Tatum, Lawrie, 47, 48, 49

About the Author

Charles L. "Chuck" Convis grew up on a North Dakota farm. He left home at sixteen to work on steam railroads in Wyoming and Utah, graduating from high school in Cheyenne. After a season on a halibut boat in the Gulf of Alaska, he joined the Marines at seventeen, fighting at Iwo Jima. He has two engineering degrees from the University of Texas. After working as a land surveyor for a Texas oil company, he entered Harvard Law School, where he received the Wall Street Journal Student Achievement Award and graduated in 1956.

His thirty-nine-year career in law included foreign oil exploration, teaching law in Texas and Pennsylvania, and serving in two California district attorney offices. During his last assignment he specialized in prosecuting murder cases. He also has a PhD in psychology and has published in law and psychology.

Chuck is the biographer of Myles Keogh of Indian Wars fame (*The Honor of Arms*, Westernlore Press, Tucson, 1990) and has published in a variety of western journals and magazines. His work has been reprinted in *Voices in Fiction and Nonfiction*. He also writes and self-publishes a series of short true sketches about the Old West, which now numbers thirty-six titles (Pioneer Press, Carson City).

Chuck and Mary Anne, his wife of sixty-two years, retired to Carson City sixteen years ago. They have five children and sixteen grandchildren, ranging in age from three to twenty-one years. He enjoys bridge, Elderhostel travel abroad, writing, and visiting grandchildren.